Beyond BETRAYAL

How God Is Healing Women (and Couples) from Infidelity

LISA TAYLOR

Foreword by Marsha Means,
co-author of *Your Sexually Addicted Spouse*

Oil of Joy
PRESS

Oil of Joy
P R E S S

Beyond Betrayal: How God Is Healing Women (and Couples) from Infidelity
Published by Oil of Joy Press
71 Lauries Dr
RD 1 Kamo 0185
New Zealand

© Lisa Taylor 2015
Cover Design: Beth Abbottsmith
Layout: Beth Abbottsmith

National Library of New Zealand Cataloguing-in-Publication entry
Author: Lisa Taylor

Title: Beyond Betrayal: How God Is Healing
Women (and Couples) from Infidelity
ISBN: 978-0-473-33798-8

Format: Softcover

Printed in Australia, 2015 – First Edition

About the 2014/2015 Survey of Wives of Sex Addicts

In mid-September 2014, the author, in conjunction with A Circle of Joy (ACOJ) ministries launched an online survey on the effects of sexual addiction on partners. Women, on the ACOJ mailing list were invited to participate. By the time the survey was closed (February 2015) 689 women had completed it. While ACOJ ministries is open to any wife/partner of a sex addict, it is estimated that the vast majority of its work is in the Christian community. Moreover, 81% of participants of the study were located in the US (5% Canada, 5% Europe, 2.5% Australia/New Zealand). More of the results from this study, and the three other smaller studies that have followed it, are discussed on the Beyond Betrayal Blog: **www.beyondbetrayal.community**

Contents

This book is dedicated to my Beloved as well as to the many beautiful sisters who have walked alongside me on this journey – including all those who shared their stories in the surveys. A special thanks goes to Marsha, Donna, Marcella, Amanda, Fonda, Sharyn, Dan, Richard and "M" for your support with this book.

Farther along we'll know more about it,
Farther along we'll understand why;
Cheer up, my [sister], live in the sunshine,
We'll understand it all by and by.

Foreword

With *Beyond Betrayal*, Lisa Taylor has done an outstanding job of tackling tough topics related to sexual addiction, particularly from a Christian perspective, for the Church at large. With boldness she has woven story and research into a practical resource. And she has not shied away from difficult topics such as:

- The differences between men's and women's brains, resulting in gender-different responses to breaks in emotional intimacy
- The Church's failure, in most cases, to provide safety, vulnerability, resources, and support within local congregations for the high percentage of marriages quietly suffering under the devastating pain of sexual addiction
- Spiritual abuse related to the way many in the church – especially spiritual leaders – advise female partners of sexual addicts.
- The difficult, and usually overlooked topic of intimacy anorexia, and the slow asphyxiation it brings to the heart and spirit, and its eventual extermination of love
- How a partner is to deal with her own sexual urges when living with intimacy anorexia
- The impact on children and the family-trauma sexual addiction produces, whether through a child's discovery of Dad's secret, or though incest.

But gratefully, Lisa does not end there. *Beyond Betrayal* is about just that: getting *beyond* the betrayal, which is where the practical enters in. Topics such as toxic lies and boundaries provide information and insight that is invaluable to the addict's partner.

Beyond Betrayal also gives us a highly beneficial chapter on intimacy, defining what it is and how to build it into one's life, even if it never happens within the framework of marriage. This chapter helps provide footholds for the millions of women who have to find ways to meet their deep, God-given need for connection that has nothing to do with their sexuality.

Thank you, Lisa, for this highly valuable resource. — Marsha Means, MA

I swipe again at the empty dispenser beside me. Turning, I peer at it with uncomprehending eyes. *Where's...?*

I look at my lap. Through the tears I'm able to make out dozens of balled up pieces of mucus-smeared toilet paper. There's more around me on the floor.

My head swivels round as a door squeaks open. I take a deep breath and hold it.

My muscles begin to ache with tension as footsteps approach. The door of the stall beside mine creaks, then slams. I close my eyes.

Please, don't let her hear me.

My nose demands my attention. Feeling around on my lap, I discover a less-used piece of TP and bring it towards my face. *Quietly, Lisa.*

My sense of shame is unbearable even without this. Having a woman ask why I'm sitting on the floor of a public toilet would be...

The tears pick up the pace.

This is so humiliating. I've never been such a sobbing wreck before.

I wipe my eyes on my sleeve, careful not to make a sound.

The toilet in the next stall flushes and I release my breath again.

Okay. I can do this. I sit a little straighter and start to clean up the mess surrounding me. It's been about 10 minutes now, time to get on with life.

10 minutes every three hours. It's a weird pattern but it's been going on for days and I can't stop it.

Of course some of these interludes of grief go on longer. Yesterday afternoon, I spent three hours in my bedroom closet huddled in a ball, sobbing as quietly as I could manage. I soaked the bed linen around me trying to muffle my sobs so that my daughter wouldn't hear me. At seven she needs to be shielded from this disaster, if possible.

Maybe I should just take her and leave now. Because really: who am I kidding? I give my marriage a 25% chance of pulling through. Maybe less.

Another marriage ripped apart by infidelity.

I put my glasses on again and stand up as the stall door beside me opens.

It's literally been the story of my life. I witnessed it as a child and I've lived through it once already as a wife. I told M while we were dating that this was the 'show stopper'. Infidelity, even as porn use, was the one thing I would not tolerate. No exceptions.

I hear the main door open and close again followed by the noise of receding footsteps. I blow my nose loudly.

I want this time to be different. My heart aches for it.

My last husband, my sons' father, had refused to get help for his problem. When I suggested couple's counselling, he said *I* was the one who needed counselling. But I wasn't the one putting porn on the computer. I wasn't the one who stayed out until after 11:00 every night of the week and disappeared frequently on weekends. It wasn't me who wouldn't answer my cell phone after 6:00 pm while 'at work'. I was just the one who'd been diagnosed with an STI at my six week post-partum check up. I hadn't even known HPV was an STI until one of the nurses at church whispered it to me one morning. I laughed. It was a misdiagnosis. It had to be!

M *only* cheats online... he says. But, who knows? My first husband lied about everything, only to come out with admissions three years after our separation (no explanation for the STI, mind you).

There's one big difference this time though. M says he wants help. He looked online and found a specialist in sexual addiction – a Christian guy. Yesterday he saw him for the first time.

A dull pain swells up in my heart and washes into my brain. Probably too little too late. My hand shakes as I flush the toilet.

Time to wash my face and finish up with the shopping. There's only five more weeks until we fly out now. The shipping container with all our household goods left the country last Sunday for our soon-to-be new home down under.

A home where I have no friends or family. A home where I know almost no one. A home where he can only meet with his new-found sex addiction counsellor over Skype.

Oh Jesus. Why didn't you let me find out sooner? Why did it have to be the same day practically everything I own set sail? I pound my fist on the stall door. I have no possessions, no job, no support and no hope.

I can't imagine ever smiling again.

CHAPTER 1

Betrayal and Trauma

If my husband had come out with the truth even five years earlier, he probably wouldn't have been able to find specialist help. There's a good chance that he would have been told by a professional that there was no such thing as a pornography 'addiction'. A secular counsellor/psychologist might even have told him that using pornography is healthy and normal.

Today, in the wake of new research on addictions, neurology and sexual health, this has changed. With society now awash in marital breakdowns, sexual dysfunction and sex crimes, there is a growing acceptance of the concept of – and term – 'sexual addiction' (SA).

Sexual Addiction and Betrayal

The definition of 'addiction' used by most mental health professionals is any compulsive behaviour that a person engages in despite the fact that it 'interferes with ordinary life responsibilities, such as work or relationships, or health.'[1] The Society for the Advancement of Sexual Health defines 'sexual addiction' as 'engaging in persistent and escalating patterns of sexual behaviour acted out despite increasing negative consequences to self and others.'[2]

While that does sound rather like what many of our husbands are caught in, some therapists and researchers will argue with the use of the word 'addiction' to describe unhealthy sexual behaviours, preferring terms such as 'hypersexual disorder' or, when the behaviour looks less compulsive, a 'sexual integrity issue'.

The debate over terminology will probably rage for years to come.[3] In this book I will talk about 'betrayal', 'infidelity', and 'sexual integrity issues'; however, most often I will use the wider, umbrella term 'sexual addiction'.[4] (A list of exact behaviours encompassed by this term follows.)

There are reasons why I favour this label. While it differs distinctly from other types of addictions, sexual addiction has much in common at least with drug addiction.[5]

In his book *Drug of the New Millennium*,[6] Mark B Kastleman describes the series of brain chemicals – including oxytocin, dopamine, and adrenaline – that are released as one views pornography. These chemicals create a 'high' much like that of cocaine or heroin. The effects of these 'superdoses' of neurochemicals are changes in the way the brain is wired.[7] Like cocaine and heroin, these blasts of neurochemicals damage the brain and impair its normal, healthy functioning. Chemical-induced brain impairment is a major reason professionals and organisations such as the National Institute on Drug Abuse (US) categorise drug addiction as a mental illness.[8]

The Downward Slide

Prolonged use of any drug – including neuro-chemicals – produces increasingly waning effects. In other words, the highs cease to be quite as high over time – due to the brain rewiring itself and certain brain receptors wearing out.

The answer? Up the dose.

For a sex addict the dose can be increased by combining sexual arousal chemicals with the chemicals released in association with emotions such as surprise, shock, anger, fear, guilt, even hopelessness. The easiest way to mix up one of these new, ultra-powerful chemical cocktails is to watch something more perverted or depraved than previously viewed. Greater highs can also be obtained through novelty (new pair of breasts) or longer exposure (hours or non-stop arousal). However, the most common route is perversion/danger – which is one of the reasons why today's paid porn is almost all 'hardcore'.

A generation ago, it wasn't easy to view hardcore porn – porn which depicts depraved activities, most commonly violence against, and humiliation of, women. Now, according to recent research, the majority of young adults have viewed homosexual intercourse (often depicted with violence) and group sex before they leave college. Similarly, over a third of our young men have witnessed porn that depicts violence/humiliation of women and bestiality by that time.[9]

Thus, it's not difficult to find something slightly 'more shocking' or perverse to expose one's brain to. Not so difficult to get that higher high. And when simply 'viewing' starts to feel passé to the acclimatised brain, one can always move to 'doing'.

Behaviours Encompassed by the Term 'Sex Addiction'

'Sexual addiction' can include habitual:

- Pornography use
- Extramarital affairs
- Use of prostitutes
- Use of strip clubs, massage parlours and other places where sexual services can be purchased
- Deviant sexual behaviour such as exhibitionism, voyeurism, fetishism
- Indulging in paraphilias: including the deviant behaviours above, as well as stimulation by the suffering or humiliation of oneself or others, children or non-consenting persons.[10]

Most of the illegal sexual behaviours that carry severe penalties – such as indecent assault, pedophilia, rape, incest – are not encompassed by the term 'sex addiction', as far as the professional treatment community is concerned. This is 'sex offending' and this category designates a much more serious illness that requires more specialised treatment.

However, because sex offending and sexual addiction tend to affect partners very similarly, the wives of sex offenders often benefit from the same kind of support as wives of addicts.

Infidelity: As We See It

As Christians we may deviate from the secular (and sometimes Christian) psychologist/counsellor and add 'habitual lusting' to this list. Women whose husbands form romantic attractions to other women on a regular basis may wonder if their husband's behaviour is encompassed by the term 'sex addiction'. While this particular manifestation of infidelity tends to be labelled 'love addiction', it is nevertheless devastating to a wife.

Dr William Struthers, one of the world's leading scientists on the effects of pornography on the brain, explains that the female brain is wired for enmeshment. This quality comes with strengths such as mental flexibility. However, it also means that emotional infidelity is as devastating, or even more so, to a woman than a physical affair with intercourse. 'A woman becomes damaged [by infidelity] in a way a man usually is not,' Struthers explains.[11]

Thus, while we may not call a man who habitually forms romantic attachments outside of his marriage a 'sex addict', his wife may very well benefit from the same supports that help wives of addicts and offenders.

As with lusting, many Christian professionals in the field of sex addiction usually have a different take on same-sex attraction: seeing it as another form of sexual brokeness, one that often (but not always) involves a sexual addiction. While this is, understandably, a controversial issue, many Christian women and men who struggle with same-sex attraction issues (whether or not they have obvious addiction symptoms) have found themselves benefitting from counselling techniques used in heterosexual sex addiction treatment.

For more on the broader issue of same-sex attraction in society, I recommend the work of Gordon Dalbey (see Resources, p. 226). For those looking for help with a same-sex attraction issue, I recommend US counsellor, Thaddeus Heffner.[12]

Treatment of Sex Addiction

A number of Christian organisations (predominantly in the US) have arisen in recent years to provide help for sex addicts. For those whose addiction is on the less extreme end of the scale, attending specialist coaching or counselling, disclosure to their spouse, support groups, doing a technology 'lock down' and finding an accountability partner will be at the core of their early recovery. Those who are more 'hard core' in their behaviours frequently do very well in classic 'addictions' treatment programmes, including live-in treatment centres. For those who show narcissistic, sociopathic or psychopathic tendencies, the help of a psychologist is generally needed: ideally one well-versed in both sexual addiction and personality disorders.

US-based Capstone Counselling says, 'Sexual addiction is a multi-dimensional problem. Treatment involves addressing *behaviours*, *emotions*, *physical changes in the brain and body*, *spirituality*, and *relationships*. For complete recovery to take place, all five of these dimensions must be addressed.'[13]

Thus, whatever our husband's 'diagnosis', and the treatment path decided on, it is crucial that treatment tackles more than just today's acting out behaviours.

Please, let's also bear in mind that labels are only useful when they help someone find a path to wholeness. They have, however, equal potential to limit a person's ability to find that wholeness: so let's be cautious in accepting any label for ourselves, or putting one on others.

Can't We Just Keep This Quiet?

Of course, the idea of taking our most socially unacceptable secrets out into the open is not palatable. Why should we seek out treatment anyway? Can't we do this at home with books and such?

Unbeknownst to those around them, most sex addicts have been trying for years to quit. Many will say, 'I've tried everything… it's just not possible for me.'

What this statement really means is, 'I've tried everything I feel comfortable with.' But, the list of things not yet tried is usually long. Often, one of the as-yet-to-be explored routes is asking friends and professionals to help. Moreover, many addicts don't trust God enough to surrender the healing process to Him. Either they don't believe God wants to, or is able to, help. Or, they are afraid of what He may ask them to do – as their part of this work of His

Why My Husband?

In my generation most men (and women) started on the road to sexual addiction as a result of trauma: generally, sexual trauma. Of the sex addicts I know (and there are now many), the ones who went deepest into their addiction were those most wounded in their sexuality as children or teens: through rape, incest, or seduction. Still other addicts were exposed in these early years to pornography (usually their father's), were the victims of sexual harassment or assault (often by other children), or had infidelity or misogyny (a low opinion of women) modelled to them.

Like all addictions, sexual addiction traps those who lack skills for coping with stress and who struggle with feelings of insecurity, shame and guilt.[14] Most addicts are slaves to more than one substance.[15]

But My Husband's a Christian!

The church has long taught that God is the answer to all our problems: including low self-worth and trauma. Yet sadly, pornography use is almost as prevalent among Christian men as non-Christian (64% compared to 65%[16]). And among Christian men who identify themselves as fundamentalists, sexual addiction is even more prevalent than in the general population.[17] Psychiatrist Dr Rory Reid gave a presentation on this disturbing subject at the 2014 IACSAS conference in Texas. The title of his talk: *Exploring Relationships of Religiosity and Hypersexual Behavior.*

So, how is it possible that Christians are just as, or more, likely to become sex addicts (or at least have sexual integrity issues) as non-Christians? Is God 'not' the answer to our problems after all?

I don't think the church is wrong in believing God is the answer. I just think the church itself sometimes doesn't know how to put people in touch with life-giving relationships. Only these kinds of relationships, with God and others, can help people deal with the terrible pain of this world, and avoid its traps. In fact, many churches (and praise God this is changing) are in the habit of heaping more guilt and shame onto people than they had before they walked through the doors. Guilt and shame are two of the key ingredients in all compulsive behaviours.

Moreover, feelings of isolation grow when we witness people being ostracised as a result of 'coming out' to their church community. They may even be expelled from the church. Indeed, it is a sad fact that many women cannot expect to receive support

from their church community once their husband's sin is known: even though they are often the number one victim of that sin.

Thus, burdened by the knowledge that they will lose their community if they show weakness, numerous men turn to 'private', easily hidden addictions such as lusting and pornography to help cope. Lusting (particularly after women in films and on TV) and pornography addiction is the gateway for other, more blatant kinds of habitual infidelity.

If your Christian husband is under the age of 40, however, there's a possibility that he did not experience trauma prior to becoming an addict: he was simply exposed to 'the drug' itself via the internet or mainstream media. The topic of cultural influencers toward sexual addiction will be discussed in Chapter 18 of this book.

That's Addicts… What About Wives?

Less than a decade ago, the wife of a man with a sexual addiction was labelled a 'co-addict' by professionals.[18] This term comes from the famous 12-step addiction-recovery model. This very worthy model spawned support programmes, such as Al-Anon for spouses of alcoholics. Al-Anon helps both wives and friends deal with the pain and trauma left in the wake of their loved-one's addiction.

As counsellors began to work with partners of alcoholics/drug addicts, they started to see destructive patterns in *their* behaviour as well. These patterns were based on the fact that the wife was supporting her husband's addiction, to his and her own detriment. This type of behaviour was labelled, 'enabling.' Partners with enabling tendencies were quickly seen as being addicted to dysfunctional relationships. Thus they became 'co-dependents'.[19]

While experts in the field will attest that the co-dependent model has been helpful in working with many partners of alcoholics and drug addicts, it has its shortcomings. Starting in the 1980's, sex addiction researchers[20] took the co-dependent theory one step further and labelled spouses 'co-addicts': stating they had a parallel addiction. This destructive label survived far longer than it should have. It is difficult to justify blanket-labelling of wives of sex addicts as co-dependent (the label given to wives of other addicts), never mind 'co-addicts'.

The shortcomings of the 'co-dependent' and 'co-addict' labels, as applied to the wife of a sex addict, become blatantly obvious when we compare her experience with the experience of the wife of an alcoholic. This woman becomes aware that her husband has an addiction fairly early in their relationship (unless she suffers from the same addiction herself). The wife of a sex addict is, in many cases, wholly unaware of her husband's addiction – at least for many years, sometimes multiple decades.

This is particularly true if she is a Christian, and as such, expects sexual integrity in her spouse. When this is the case, he will hide his behaviour well. With no smell on his breath, wobble in his walk, dilated pupils, erratic behaviour (other than some disappearances), how is she to identify the problem on her own? In the case of a single affair, or being caught out once at the computer, how is she to identify the behaviour as habitual?

If the wife cannot perceive a destructive, habitual behaviour, how can she enable it?[21] One SA counsellor told me that subconsciously, we wives do actually 'know'. I disagree. Having already been in a marriage to one sex addict (who I caught, thanks to God revealing evidence I wasn't even looking for), I was naturally more suspicious and alert to the signs than most women of my generation. Still, I was fooled twice. 'Shame on me', as the saying goes.

In my defence I have to say that I chose not to be a jealous, suspicious person. I chose the path of trust. (Before I knock myself over, with these pats on the back, I'll admit I also chose to turn a blind eye to some other serious character flaws.)

Even so, I showed some caution and thus, on two occasions, when I felt in my spirit that something was wrong, I asked M directly if he had been using pornography. He lied and said, 'No!'

Sometimes I feel I failed myself by choosing to believe him; but I certainly did not fail God. Nor do I deserve a demeaning label for believing what I was told when there was no evidence to the contrary.

As one wise ex-pastor's wife (and wives' support coach) put it, "You're never just dealing with sex addiction. You're also dealing with an addiction to lies and deception."[22] The fact that our husband is lying to us and living a double life is, at times, more painful than the actual betrayal. This pain is only increased if we are told that we actually 'did know' about this other life.

....

> I have had three severe anxiety attacks. After the first one was witnessed by my children, I began to keep a paper bag in my nightstand drawer. — survey respondent

....

Post Traumatic Stress Disorder

So if we are not all co-dependents[23] or co-addicts… what is wrong with us? Our behaviours have become – well, not the model of perfect mental health. Surely the erratic, unhealthy actions exhibited by thousands of betrayed wives need some explanation.

Thankfully, in 2005 Dr Barbara Steffens began formulating what would become known as the 'Multidimensional Partner Trauma Model' (M-PTM), which brought to light the traumatic impact of the discovery of sex addiction, and its related behaviours, on the partner/spouse. A similar model was developed simultaneously by Dr Omar Minwalla.[24]

In 2009, Steffens and Marsha Means, MA published a book that made M-PTM accessible to women outside of academic circles. The book, *Your Sexually Addicted Spouse*,[25] has flown off the shelves of booksellers around the world. Many, myself included, have considered it nothing short of a Godsend.

From the book we learn that wives' reactions to their husbands' addiction can be understood as safety-seeking responses. In other words, we experience trauma when we become aware of our husband's infidelity – most particularly when we discover it on our own. This results in our feeling threatened, wounded and vulnerable. These feelings cause the majority of us to become obsessive safety-seekers and pain-avoiders. Techniques we begin to employ vary from denial to over-controlling, but all fail to dodge the extreme psychological distress for long.

In a survey I conducted in conjunction with A Circle of Joy ministries in 2014/2015, 98% of the nearly 700 respondents reported feeling they had suffered some degree of trauma following discovery of their husband's infidelity/sexual addiction. The top symptoms experienced were anger/rage (88%); intrusive, negative thoughts (84%), interrupted sleep (80%), mental confusion (75%) and extreme negative feelings about self (73%).

So next time we find ourself asking, 'What is wrong with me?' We can listen to the advice of Dr Sheri Keffer: 'I tell partners, it's not something wrong in you, it's that something bad happened to you. You are a trauma survivor.'[26]

The goal of this book is to help you (and possibly your husband) find your way past the trauma and into the fullness of life God has for you.

Taking it Further

Read the following statements and meditate on them:

- My husband's addiction is not my fault: he would have done this no matter whom he'd married.
- I have the right to be brokenhearted and grief-stricken
- I have the right to be angry
- I have the right to be mentally confused (not as 'with it' as normal)
- I have the right to feel physically ill
- I have the right to cry
- It is normal in my circumstances to:
  - » Wake up feeling panicked
  - » Sleep only a few hours per night
  - » Eat less (or eat more)
  - » Become sweaty, panicky and have difficulty breathing in public, or in the presence of other women, pornography or suggestive media
  - » Find it difficult to get out of bed
  - » Feel like I have nothing left to live for (at times)
  - » Feel I am ugly, stupid, insignificant, not in control, at fault
  - » Feel the need to try and control the world around me
  - » Feel angry at God
  - » Be short-tempered
  - » Distrust specific people, possibly everyone
  - » Startle more frequently/more dramatically
- I have the right, and would be well advised, to seek out specialist support for myself alone (not just couple support).

> For Reflection Psalm 31

Endnotes

1   *Psychology Today*, 'Psych Basics: Addiction', Retrieved February 2014, <http://www..com/basics/addiction>.

2   SASH, 'Sexual Addiction Treatment and Recovery'. Retrieved January 2014, <www.abridgetorecovery.com/what-we-treat/sex-addiction.html>.

3   An excellent look at the debate can be found in the free Covenant Eyes PDF, 'Fight Porn in Your Church' by Luke Gilkerson.

4   Such as peeping, exhibitionism, illegal soliciting. Sadly there is a wide range of sex offending today.

5   However drug addiction is said to be a substance addiction and sexual addiction is referred to by professionals as a process addiction.

6   PowerThink Publishing, 2007.

7   WM Struthers, *Wired for Intimacy: How Pornography Hijacks the Male Brain,* InterVarsity Press, 2009.

8   National Institute on Drug Abuse, 'Comorbidity: Addiction and Other Mental Illnesses', Retrieved April, 2014, < http://1.usa.gov/1AetzSn >.

9   C Sabina, J Wolak, and D Finkelhor, 'The Nature and Dynamics of Internet Pornography Exposure for Youth,' *CyberPsychology and Behavior* vol 11, 2008 pp. 691-693.

10 *Psychology Today*, 'Sexual Perversions', Retrieved March 2014, <http://www.psychologytoday.com/blog/great-sex/200806/sexual-perversions>.

11 WM Struthers, IACSAS: Redeeming Sexuality and Intimacy conference, 2014.

12 Thaddeus Heffner, www.thaddeusheffner.com. Wives may benefit from coaching with Journey to Healing and Joy coach, Sarah Fletcher <http://journeytohealingandjoy.com>.

13 D Meredith-Dixon, *A Door of Hope*, 2015, quoted from http://capstoneatlanta.com/?page_id=395 Retrieved August 29, 2015.

14   Some people describe these traps as HALT: hungry, angry, lonely, tired.

15   Moreover, it is more than substances that trap us:
        consider gambling, media, romances.

16   Proven Men Ministries, '2014 Pornography Survey and Statistics', Retrieved
        Dec. 29, 2014 <http://www.provenmen.org/2014pornsurvey/>.

17   91% according to Steven Stack, Ira Wasserman, and Roger Kern:
        'Adult Social Bonds and Use of Internet Pornography.' *Social Science
        Quarterly* 85 (March 2004): pp. 75-88. Some experts such as Dr
        Struthers believe that to some extent over-reporting may influence
        this number as well as 'under-reporting' in the secular community.

18   Labels such as co-addict and co-dependent are still very
        commonly used by therapists down under (and in other parts
        of the world), who seem to lag behind the North American
        therapy community in terms of education in this area.

19   For more on this model see *Codependendent No More*, Melody Beattie.

20   P Carnes, *Don't Call it Love,* Bantam, 1992.

21   That said, it's not uncommon to find women enabling some form of
        dysfunction in their families. This however is a complex issue which may
        involve habituation to dysfunction, religious views around submission, and
        the amount of support she has within and outside the family. Blanket labels:
        never do justice to complex human dynamics. That includes the 'addict' label.

22   K Brockman, "Spiritual Crisis: Episode 3," Marsha Means
        Podcast series, www.beyondbetrayal.community.

23   This is not to say that some wives of sex addicts do not display co-dependent
        traits. Some do. Some strongly so. However, this does not mean that a co-
        dependent label or current co-dependent 'treatment' models will help them.

24   D Meredith-Dixon, ibid.

25   New Horizon Press, 2009.

26   S Keffer, 'The Trauma of Sexual Betrayal', New Life TV, April 27, 2014.

It's 3:00 am and I am curled up in a ball on the floor again. The carpet beneath me is soaked with tears. Waves of nausea roll over me as I rock and pray. It's been two weeks since M's first disclosure of pornography use (others have followed) and I've lost 4kg. The pain in my stomach is constant.

I'm having trouble focusing as I pray.

Finally my thoughts move to Jesus: to *his* pain. I picture him on the cross, beaten, gashed, bloody, arms and shoulders dislocated.

As I reflect on his suffering I think about the onlookers. In my imagination I can see standing in front of him, a couple hundred metres away, an army of hideous spectres. They are mocking Him, jeering and firing arrows: arrows of shame, rejection, despair, humiliation. The Lord Almighty has, in love, made himself vulnerable.

This assault is humanity's – and His enemies – response to that vulnerability.

Like a baby animal, unable to leave its dying mother, I imagine I am standing beside him: a child of maybe 4. One arm is wrapped around his bleeding calf. The other arm is lifting my thumb to my mouth. I cling to him.

I am beaten too, and starved and wretched. I am covered in blood, but it is His blood. Stray arrows, aimed at Him, graze me. I don't move. Where else can I go? Finally an arrow pierces my chest. In terror I seek out His face. I can feel the poison – rejection and humiliation – beginning to spread into my lungs.

Agony. His face is contorted by it, but His eyes... His eyes. What love, what patience. I can read the sorrow there – sorrow, incredibly, for me and *my* pain.

Realisation dawns: my pain is a by-product of His. He understands it. He has lived it... and far more. He cares.

He is modelling for me how to walk through pain beyond bearing.

I feel the poison beginning to recede. He is drawing it into Himself – where it will be destroyed.

CHAPTER 2
Effects of Trauma

It can be a relief to learn that we haven't lost our minds – that we are traumatised, not lunatics. However, that knowledge alone isn't going to ease the pain in our hearts or make our day-to-day lives more manageable. There are still the problems listed in the meditation section of the last chapter: a list which is far from definitive.

And, too often, just as we are making progress with those issues, we learn something new about our husband's betrayal. We find we've been lied to, or encounter a 'trigger' – an event or situation which reminds us of the betrayal and brings the sense of danger sweeping in. Such events can knock us right back to where we started. In this chapter we will look briefly at why we know the trauma model is accurate, how trauma works in us, what emotions we might be facing because of our trauma and, finally, solutions for trauma's unmanageable, debilitating emotions.

....

I couldn't go to the mall for a long time because of all the images and I'd start to panic. I became hypersensitive to images of scantily clad women. Also high heel shoes would trigger me because I thought of strippers.

— survey respondent

....

Trauma? As If…

At least one psychologist[27] – and he's almost certainly not alone – scoffs at the the idea of the term PTSD being applied to the wives of sex addicts. Then again, he also scoffs at the term 'sexual addiction'. He claims that in order for a woman to have a traumatic stress reaction, such as one that causes PTSD, her life (i.e., her physical existence) needs to have been threatened, such as it might be in a rape situation.

Many of us could tell him that we not only felt our life (i.e., life as we'd known it) threatened when we discovered our husband's infidelity, we felt brutally assaulted – almost to the point of death. Many men may see this as a stretch.[28] Not so the women who have experienced betrayal.

And while most men find it difficult, if not impossible, to 'get' the utter emotional and psychological devastation sexual addiction causes an unsuspecting wife, some do. Another psychologist[29] commented online to the aforementioned scoffer saying that while he personally doesn't know if a wife's reaction fits perfectly into the PTSD model, in his practice he has seen women recover more easily from rape than from betrayal.[30] A number of women who have experienced both (along with other horrific traumas) replied to say they felt this was true.

One wife wrote:

I've been raped. Rape is at least a time-limited event, and there are things you can do to enhance your feelings of safety. I'm living with this [my husband's addiction], day in and day out, no sense of safety in sight. And I have to keep it together, for my kids. There are very few supports for me, most of them cost money. We don't have a lot of money… I'd choose rape over this any day of the week. It's terrifying, but I don't have to figure out how to build a life with my rapist.[31]

Another woman commented that one of the measures of PTSD, in the DSM (Diagnostic and Statistical Manual: the guidebook of mental health disorders for professionals in the US) lists 19 possible criteria for identifying PTSD. Her psychologist identified 17 of the 19 in her – far more than is needed to receive a diagnosis of PTSD.

Whether we call the devastation women experience PTSD, or some new term, it makes little difference to us women. Labels are limited. Where they become important is in understanding how best to help and support the hurting. The woman identified with 17 of the PTSD criteria said she has benefited greatly from being treated with the best practices used to aid trauma victims – whereas no prior treatment had helped her.

I believe that what I experienced following my husband's admission of his betrayal is best described by the PTSD model. I'm aware of numerous others who say the same – including 98% of the 2014/2015 Survey respondents. As Marsha Means so aptly put it in her first book on betrayal: 'Discovering emotional or physical infidelity is a form of death. . . . [She] can no longer turn to him with the certainty that he will value and protect the intimacy [they] shared. . . . [Her] loss is real and it slices [her] soul.'[32]

I couldn't quit crying. — survey respondent

Trauma: What it Does

So why is our soul sliced? Why is our husband's betrayal so debilitating for most of us? In her workbook for betrayed spouses, Means writes: 'You have experienced relational trauma because the deep attachment bond shared with your partner was broken. Relational trauma is considered the most excruciating emotional pain we can feel.'[33]

One of the effects of this pain is that we lose the ability to self-soothe in healthy ways. Says renowned PTSD researcher, Dr Bessel van der Kolk,

'Instead they [traumatised people] tend to rely on actions such as fight or flight or pathological self-soothing (for example mutilation, binging, starving or turning to alcohol and drugs) to regulate their internal balance.'[34]

Other unhealthy soothing methods I have known betrayed wives to turn to include over-shopping, affairs, erotica/romance novels, TV, over-eating, over-working/ volunteering. (See more in Chapter 10.)

However, 80% of respondents to the 2014/2015 Survey stated that drawing closer to God helped them with their healing. This is the perfect time to learn to make God our refuge: the one we run to when the pain of life becomes unbearable. This new pattern of soothing is not going to happen overnight, but it can happen with regular practice. This doesn't mean finding comfort only in the bible. God has many ways to engage us and speak to us: conversational prayer,[35] scripture, music/worship, nature, creative pursuits, and our sisters and brothers in community. For myself, I didn't start off with a particularly 'up close and personal' relationship with God, but I have developed one. I now refer to Him as 'Abba', and my relationship with Him is the one I most cherish.

More on healthy soothing techniques follow at the end of this chapter.

Trauma on Trauma

The sad reality of life in this broken world is that many of us were victims of trauma long before we discovered we'd been betrayed by our spouses. 'The majority of spouses have sexual, emotional, physical or spiritual abuse in their past,' writes International Association of Certified Sexual Addiction Specialists (IACSAS) President, Richard Blankenship in *Spouses of Sex Addicts: Hope for the Journey*.[36] If trauma is not, however in their past, the trauma of being the partner of a sex addict will be devastating enough, Blankenship adds.[37]

Therapists talk of two major groups of trauma that can harm people: Type A and Type B. Type A trauma are 'invasive trauma' – that is external forces that invade our lives. It includes physical, emotional, sexual and spiritual trauma. Type B trauma refers to deficit-based trauma: where a regular deficiency of love, attention, safety, information, etc. causes the wound.

When we experience a very extreme form of trauma, such as the betrayal of our spouse, it is likely going to bring back memories and pain from past traumas. This may even include traumas we felt had been resolved.

While this 'trauma compounded by more trauma' can be incredibly crippling for a time, our Redeemer can do something with this. 'The impact of trauma is more devastating than you might have previously imagined. This is a time to begin healing old wounds as well as new ones,' writes Blankenship.[38] However, he stresses that the current wounds must be the first priority.[39]

While that may sound a bit optimistic to those in the early crisis phase of the journey, many wives, myself included, relate that they felt able to 'delve into' past traumas at new levels as they worked on their betrayal trauma. That result was not influenced by whether or not the marriage improved, or even survived.

I felt like I was walking around in shock for about three months. — survey respondent

Sorrow Meets Shock

Blankenship has said of grief, 'Spouses of sex addicts suffer "shock grief" upon discovery of the pornography, affair partner, or whatever form the addiction takes.'

This term captures beautifully the pain of the combined sorrow and shock wives of addicts experience on learning they are betrayed. Shock grief is often described by women in the terminology of graphic violence. Many of us feel we've been brutally, physically assaulted without cause or warning.

The result of shock grief is sorrow, anger, and fear. Any one of these emotions – many hours of the day and night spent weeping with sorrow, for example – will make our lives exceedingly challenging. The combination of the three, and the usual emotional 'see-sawing' between them, can rob us of our ability to cope. It even challenges our ability to reach out to God and others, as we so desperately need to at this time.

In the next chapter we'll break down these three emotions and look at how women are coping with them… or not.

Taking it Further

A husband's infidelity is a betrayal on numerous levels: betrayal of our attachment bond (the intimacy of our relationship), betrayal of our marriage vows, betrayal of our children, betrayal of our trust, betrayal of his role (where this belief is held) as supporter and/or protector. Each betrayal brings with it an immense amount of pain.

Donna Meredith-Dixon, in *A Door of Hope*, writes: 'Though we wish God would simply put an end to suffering, at least for the time being God's approach to suffering is not to end it, but to enter it. Like it or not, our best hope in this often broken world is to find refuge in God's presence.'[40]

- Journal a prayer to God about which betrayals are most painful right now and why.
- Write a poem, a song, or draw/paint a picture that expresses your pain right now. Use another creative medium if that suits better.
- Sing/play a song or recite a psalm that captures some of your pain.

For Reflection Psalm 34, particularly verses 17-22

Endnotes

27   DJ Ley, 'Abusing the Term Trauma: Can "my partner cheated on me" really be called traumatic?' *Psychology Today*, Sept 20, 2012, viewed March 2014, < http://bit.ly/1DnXO7M>.

28   Lacking the enmeshment wiring of the female brain (Dr Struthers told his 2014 IACSAS workshop attendees) many men reason that so long as 'his penis didn't enter her vagina,' there was no infidelity. Jesus' take on this question falls squarely on the side of us women: to lust is to commit adultery.

29   Ley, ibid, viewed March, 2014. <http://www.psychologytoday.com/blog/women-who-stray/201209/abusing-the-term-trauma/comments>.

30   It was the original author of the article (Ley) who made the comparison between rape ('real trauma,' he said) and betrayal by a SA husband ('not trauma').

31   Anonymous comment to the article by DJ Ley, ibid, retrieved March, 2014. <www.psychologytoday.com/blog/women-who-stray/201209/abusing-the-term-trauma/comments>.

32   M Means, *Living with your Husband's Secret Wars, F.H. Revell*, Grand Rapids, Michigan,1999, p 125.

33   M Means, *Journey to Healing and Joy*, p. 21.

34   B Van der Kolk, 'In Terror's Grip'. Quoted from *Your Sexually Addicted Spouse*, p. 143.

35   My favourite book on conversational (i.e. two-way) prayer is *Whispers of My Abba* by David Takle.

36   R Blankenship, *Spouses of Sex Addicts: Hope for the Jouney*, Xulon Press, 2010, p. 39.

37   Blankenship, email interview, September 21, 2015.

38   Blankenship, ibid. p. 39.

39   Blankenship, interview.

40   Meredith-Dixon, ibid, preface.

'My fault?'

'Yeah. I told you to go online and order yourself a new pair of pyjamas.' M's eyes, defiant up until this point, now glance at my hand and I see his smug expression vanish. He looks uneasy.

I glance at my hand. Oh right. I'm still holding the chopping knife I'd been using to cut carrots when my inner lightbulb came on. I hadn't actually meant to bring it with me...

From the doorway of the bedroom I use it to point at him. 'So, you're going to sit there and tell me that you used buying me a birthday present as a chance to act out? And this is *my* fault? Why don't you just say it was my fault for having a birthday.'

M is almost literally squirming now. He's clearly not going to say anything more while I'm holding the knife. I go to the kitchen and slam the utensil down on the cutting board. As I do so, I look across into the living room.

That *&%#@$ computer. I stride over to it, snatch up the modem and smash it onto the floor. A rather satisfying sound of broken plastic and electronics greets my ears. 'There we go,' I call out. 'Problem solved. No more internet.'

I notice my daughter staring wide-eyed from the corner of the living room where she'd been playing. Shame and grief wash over me. She's going to think I've lost my mind. If only she knew.

My husband walks into the room, his mouth hanging open. I nail him with my eyes. 'Don't you blame *me* for your problems. And don't ever buy me a birthday present again. Ever!'

CHAPTER 3

Managing the Unmanageable

Sorrow, anger, fear. These are three of the most debilitating emotions women encounter as a result of their husband's betrayal and the resulting trauma. Sorrow, probably the fundamental feeling behind anger, will be looked at in detail in Chapter 11, along with depression and suicidal ideation. If this is your predominant struggle, you may wish to skip to that chapter now.

Anger

One of the manifestations of overwhelming sorrow is anger. When sorrow can find no validation, no healthy outlet, it will commonly begin to fester until rage comes bubbling out.

70% of the women who responded to the 2014/2015 Survey admitted doing something they regretted in response to discovering their husband's betrayal. The single most common regret was lashing out verbally. The second most common: lashing out physically.[41] 'I smashed a few cell phones, a computer, and a PlayStation with a sledge hammer,' one woman admitted. One of the women I have supported over the years – a pastor's wife (now ex-wife) – said, 'The day I found out about R and the prostitutes, was the day I started swearing.'

Normally very mild tempered women can find themselves, in the initial trauma crisis, experiencing incredible amounts of rage. This is to be expected and is not cause for concern as long as the rage is directed appropriately and recedes as stress levels decline.

Of course what exactly 'appropriate direction' is for rage is up for debate. I personally feel the average husband can stand being verbally attacked, even sworn at, occasionally without too much difficulty. An apology at some point would be appropriate in most cases. However, if our anger is being turned towards others (especially our children) or if a frequent pattern of yelling and raging begins to emerge: it's time to seek help.

After a short episode of yelling at her sex offender husband, the third one of its kind in 12 months, N said to me. 'I feel so bad. I was really mean. But in that moment, I knew nothing else would satiate my anger.'

'You feel bad because this isn't the real you. It was the emotions overwhelming you.' I went on to give her the statistic, from the survey about how common this issue is and that it's listed as a 'regret'.

Then she asked me a rather surprising question: 'If it's so natural, why do women say they regret it after? I think it was actually good for my husband to see how much he'd hurt me, because normally he just doesn't get it.'

This is a good question really. Moreover, I've also witnessed that the light doesn't go on for some husbands until they see a very uncharacteristic display of anger. So I spent some time that night trying to think the 'regret' aspect through. The best answer I came up with was 'culture'.

I lived in an Italian-immigrant neighbourhood during university. Blowouts between family members echoed up and down the street fairly regularly. The next day, the people would usher forth from the same house the walls were shaking in the night before. There'd be kissing, hugging, hand-holding and great peals of laughter and joviality. I realised that as much as what they'd done was unacceptable in my 'stiff upper lip' culture, to them, grand shows of emotion – positive and negative – were normal.

Attending a tangi (Maori funeral service) last year, I witnessed the same thing: huge displays of emotion, this time, grief. Not only did the emotion seem natural in this context, it struck me as potentially healing.

Our conservative western-European culture, however, often looks askance at such displays. I've noticed that older generations, in particular, disapprove of verbal expressions of anger. This is true amongst therapists as well, with older therapists tending to have a stance of 'never acceptable', and the younger ones saying something more along the lines of, 'Suck it up, husbands… though you can duck if she throws something.'[42]

Thus, while our feelings of shame around 'losing it' are complex, I think some of the bigger factors at work are living in a culture that values emotional repression, the fact that many 'experts' tell women this behaviour is shameful, and of course, our understanding that 'this isn't who I am!'

In any case, there is One to whom we can take our shame and receive healing and forgiveness. As it turns out: He experienced some pretty big emotions himself, and let them out. He does understand our pain.

....

> I said horrible things to him, called him names, and threw a coffee cup across the room in a rage. I hate the rages they scare me and I feel like a bad person.
>
> — survey respondent

....

Violence

My husband would (due to his particular issues) occasionally offer for me to hit him when I was angry. I almost always declined, but a couple of times I took him up on it – with the result that I hurt my fist hitting his chest but did him no damage. (Note: my husband is considerably larger than I am and, using only my body, I stand no chance of hurting him. I was fully aware of this the times I lashed out).

Though this story shocks some people, it has actually helped many too: generally those who have had the occasional violent outburst. In the same way, the last time I hit my husband (this one was uninvited) a sister told me the next day of the physical tussles she's had with her addict/narcissist husband. My reaction was, 'Phew, it's not just me.'

I am not recommending here that any woman use physical violence on her spouse (and trust me, I am not proud of having descended to that level). However, if this is part of your story – and the survey results show it *is* part of many of our stories – I do ask that you seek God's forgiveness and move on. Like the verbal anger, if we notice violence becoming a regular pattern, we can seek professional help. Also, if we have ever been seriously tempted to use a weapon (or any object) to inflict bodily harm on our spouse (or anyone), we need to contact a specialist as soon as possible. Let's not be too ashamed to seek help – this is what trauma can do. It doesn't have to define us.

Let's remember that whenever the anger threatens to overcome us, we can call out to our Abba in heaven and remove ourself from the situation (if possible). Other techniques for calming ourselves are the same as the self-soothing techniques listed at the end of this chapter.

Overall, rage should naturally subside as we find support and progress on our healing journey. In particular, we can learn not to link our sense of safety with our husband's fidelity (as impossible as that may seem initially). As God increasingly becomes our refuge, we will increasingly live in a place of peace.

Fears and Anxiety

One of the main factors alienating us from God and others at this time is fear born of mistrust. It is not surprising that when we are betrayed by the one to whom we made ourselves most vulnerable, the one to whom we trusted the safety of our body and soul, we find ourselves asking if there is anyone left we *can* trust. An overwhelming distrust of most everyone, including God, is part of the debilitating fear most of us face. Other fears include fear of future betrayals, fear for our own and our children's safety, fear we don't have the full truth, fear of financial ruin, fear of disease, fear of exposure and humiliation, and fear of our own wild emotions and reactions.

While we are right not to implicitly trust our spouses at this point, it is helpful to our healing if we give God a chance to prove Himself to us. Blankenship writes:

'This is a journey that will change your relationship with God. At times it will feel like faith is worthless. At other times it may feel like the only thing you have to hang onto. You may question the very existence of God. You are in good company. Many great men and women throughout the bible had doubts, and their faith was strengthened anyway.'[43]

Many of those men and women, I would add, also found healing for their traumas, as documented in scripture.

No one understands trauma and grief quite like Jesus. He is the one to whom all honour was due, and yet on whom humanity inflicted all manner of traumas, including betrayal, abandonment, physical abuse and murder. He *does* understand and is very patient with our natural reactions to trauma: including fear and anger. Let's not be afraid to have a brutally honest conversation with God about where we are at with our fears and our trust. We can journal this conversation if we have trouble keeping our mind focused enough to pray. Then, let's be open to His overtures of love and comfort. Numerous women I know have been shocked to:

- Feel themselves physically hugged
- Receive a supernatural sign of love
- Be lead to a scripture that instantly comforted
- In other ways experience God actively reaching out to them at this time

While we are 'tasting' and 'seeing' that the Lord is good, we can ask Him to help steer us toward people to whom we can safely share our story.[44] That's a tall order. There are far more unsafe people than safe ones out there. However, the natural instinct to withdraw (affecting most spouses) will only take us so far: it will help us avoid unsafe people, but it won't take us to the needed safe ones. That's where prayer and some knowledge can go a long way.

My hope is that you are already more able to identify safe people than you were before you started reading this book.

....

> I did not, and still do not, enjoy anything in life like I did before. — survey respondent

....

Overcoming Fear and Other Unmanageable Emotions

Above, I have mentioned some key techniques for managing our fears.

- Praying
- Journaling
- Finding safe people with whom to share our story
- Seeking out a therapist
- Worshipping God (playing music/singing) and quiet time with Him
- Creating: writing a poem, a song, painting or drawing
- Seeking knowledge: through quality books and online resources

Others I didn't mention include exercising, practicing 'being present' with others, avoiding triggers, taking warm baths, making positive dietary changes, getting a massage, having a spa day, listening to a 'soaking prayer'. If we find ourself succuming to a panic attack, we can turn to 'grounding' exercises like tracing the shape of our fingers.[45]

Many of these techniques were mentioned by the women who participated in the 2014/2015 Survey as ones which helped them to cope with their pain. For more ideas on ways to self-sooth, I recommend reading Chapter 7 of Means' and Steffens' *Your Sexually Addicted Spouse*.

These techniques also work for anger and other strong, debilitating emotions. There are other tools that I have not listed here but which will be dealt with in subsequent chapters. These include support groups, visualising 'God with you' (Immanuel Prayer), setting boundaries, seeking out full disclosure, starting the forgiveness process and practicing emotional detachment.

> I lost my menstrual cycle for nine months.
>
> — survey respondent

Overcoming Health-Related Fears

When it comes to the fear of disease, a check for STIs (formerly 'STDs') is an absolute must for every spouse of a sex addict. Many women have been told, 'It was just pornography', or some other non-contact form of sexual addiction/betrayal only to find they were carrying an STI. It can feel very humiliating to ask our doctor for a full battery of STI testing. One option, to help us better cope, would be to take a trusted friend with us to the appointment.

Also, it is normal to experience weight loss in the early trauma crisis. I went down two clothing sizes in the first month: this despite forcing myself to eat when I didn't want to. However, I gained the weight back over the next 12 months without taking any particular action.

More disturbing, however, are signs of an auto-immune disorder (or aggravation of an existing one). I already had celiac disease, and despite eating my usual gluten-free diet, saw my body react as if I were wolfing down a loaf of wheat bread at every meal. Other women experience allergy flare ups, skin eruptions, arthritic pains – even severe, unaccountable muscle spasms. Many of these physical ailments will scale back as a woman's stress levels decrease. However, don't hesitate to see a doctor or natural health practitioner if these health issues are becoming too disruptive to life or do not recede with time and the lessening of stress.

The Pharmaceutical Debate

Of the women I know personally who have taken prescription medicine for their anxiety, sleeplessness and depression, only a few were glad they did. I know many more who took them and were extremely unhappy with at least some of the results.

One example is K who started on the threesome of sleeping pills, anti-anxiety medication and anti-depressants after her first suicide attempt (related to domestic violence and betrayal). They worked well for a few months, but then she made another attempt on her life. This was followed by two more. Eventually she realised that the 'voices in her head' urging her to end it were now far more persistent than before she went on medication. After some research on the internet she decided to take herself off her medication.[46] It was a very difficult process with a lot of withdrawal symptoms. Ultimately, however, she was relieved to be off the drugs, noting that her suicidal ideations were vastly reduced. She also noticed that she had large gaps in her memory from the time she was on the medicine.

K was fortunate to find she was able to get off the drugs. A friend, L, feels her brain chemistry has become so upset by medication that not only have her symptoms worsened (after a short-lived, initial improvement), but that she is now completely unable to reduce the medication without serious aggravation to her anxiety, etc. She feels trapped.

Other women have reported feeling constantly stoned while on medication, with at least one woman I know (a medical professional) having had a psychotic episode, after starting on anti-depressants, that resulted in her losing her job. Another woman of my acquaintance became unable (after starting anti-depressants) to monitor a dangerous situation at home. The result: her daughter was lured into her husband's activity (it took her support group pointing out the signs to her). When the girl's behaviour became public, the teen then tried to commit suicide using mum's sleeping pills.

Still others, such as A, find that they miss the signs of what is really going on with their husband's recovery while on medication. Within days of quitting her anti-depressant,

A realised her husband's stories weren't quite adding up and challenged him. His reaction, when pushed, was to finally confess (in an angry and abusive manner) that he was still acting out (illegally).

When she responded with anger to this information, A's husband tried to convince her (and others) she was having a psychotic episode and needed to return to her medication.[47] She instead turned to God, then to other women. A sat through one couple's session with her husband and realised that the lying, spiritualising, manipulation and acting out hadn't actually improved much in two years and it was time to take firm action.

In the natural world the purpose of pain is to motivate us to make a change.

I myself prefer natural therapies, and so sought out (in addition to the above self-soothing techniques) complementary medicine to help with my grief-shock and ensuing emotional turmoil. I state this in order to make my personal bias on the issue clear.

The pharmaceutical question is a very touchy subject: both in the church and outside it. Let me state very clearly, that while I did not take prescription medication – and when I'm asked, do caution women – I believe every woman's choice on this matter must be respected. A woman is not 'spiritually weak' if she chooses to take sleeping pills, anti-anxiety drugs or anti-depressants. She is overwhelmed.

The majority of women who make it through this journey without medication display extremely good self-care and often are in a position to slow down. Most women I know who went on pharmaceuticals were working full-time (at the point of the trauma crisis) and had otherwise busy lives: raising children, volunteering, etc. Moreover, they had little support and validation for their trauma.

The few women I know who have successfully navigated pharmaceutical use had doctors who:

- Didn't exceed maximum recommended dosages (as L's doctor did)
- Saw the drugs as a temporary measure
- Would not readily prescribe sleeping pills, anti-depressants and anti-anxiety drugs in tandem

If we are a person who believes God's children should not be using medication to control the pain in their lives, that's fine. However, we should, then, also be a person willing to support others in their hour of need. If we do this – you and I – out of love and compassion, then we will prove ourselves to be the Body of Christ: a church living up to its high calling. I suspect on the way, our principles (such as whether it's 'right' to take medication) will become less important than His people.

What a Husband Can Do to Help

Both in his excellent book, *Worthy of Her Trust: What you Need to Do to Rebuild Trust* and his *Kitchen Convo* video series, sex addiction therapist Jason Martinkus gives men advice that may help circumvent the worst of their wife's anger, and help her overcome her fears.

Martinkus talks about the need for men, who are invested in healing the relationship, to make a 'safe container' for their wives to share their pain. He adds,

'And you need to be a willing recipient of it. I try to help guys understand that all those questions is grieving... being arrogant, being defensive, getting hung up on the technicalities, shuts down the grieving process. You have to let her get that stuff out and ask those questions.'

In Chapter 16 we will also talk about Martinkus' amends matrix, which can go a long way to helping women grieve in healthier ways, and from there, heal.

Taking it Further

Write a letter to your spouse about your feelings around his betrayal. Don't hold back anything. Search your heart and use whatever language best expresses your pain. Save this letter in a journal or destroy it in some way that feels cathartic (beat it with a stick, tear it up and toss it to the wind, make a bonfire and burn it).

Alternatively, draw or paint a picture of yourself at this moment, or a picture of your spouse the way you now see him.

Write a letter to God about how you're feeling at this moment. If you're feeling let down by Him or angry with Him, don't hold back on expressing this. God knows our hearts better than we do ourselves, so we aren't going to shock Him.

Imagine the 'worst case scenario' for you and your family. Think about things you could do to cope. What could you live without (be brutally honest: we can live without quite a lot in reality, we're just frequently unwilling to). What things could you acquire in creative ways (e.g., could you carpool, borrow a car temporarily from a family member, take public transport)? Reflect on your list and remember that God has promised to be your provider.

The next time you feel yourself overwhelmed by anxiety, put on a 'soaking prayer'. There are many available free online, including 'Rise Up a Warrior', by Graham Cooke. There are also some that can be purchased for a very reasonable cost, e.g., 'Psalm 91' by Australian, David Tensen: davidtensen.com

> *For Reflection*: Does God 'get' our anger and pain? Read and reflect on Ezekiel 16. Read Psalm 77. Can you follow the psalmist's general pattern with your prayer?

Endnotes

41 The majority of these respondents confessed to physically attacking their husbands, but some limited their rage to destroying property. Numerous other women stated they regretted contemplating physical violence and a handful mentioned taking out their anger on their husband's mistress/the sex worker.

42 This adapted quote comes from therapist Jason Martinkus, *Kitchen Conversation* series, viewed September 2014 <http://newlife.com/emb/tag/kitchen-conversations/>.

43 Blankenship, ibid, p. 34.

44 Marsha Means in her plenary presentation at the IACSAS conference May 2014 suggests: 'share a little bit of your story. See if she shares back. If so, you know she's safe.'

45 For more on grounding techniques, see Beyond Betrayal Blog: 'Triggered' <http://beyondbetrayal.community/triggered-2/>.

46 Please note that rapid, self-regulated cessation of such drugs often leads to severe withdrawal symptoms and is not recommended by health practitioners.

47 A's medication was an anti-depressant, not an anti-psychotic. She had no history of psychotic episodes, nor was she having one at that moment.

I lie on top of the covers rather than under them. It is probably 24 degrees, at midnight but I am shaking violently, as if it were the middle of winter. Nearby, my little girl sleeps on a futon. My sons are on the other side of the room each in a bed and my husband lies next to me.

We have travelled a long way to get to this B&B... halfway across the country. Tomorrow my nearly adult sons return to their visit with their biological father: whose story they were told yesterday. They've also been made aware of their step-father's story and have in return confessed their own, far less serious, struggles around purity. There have been many tears, prayers, and meetings with a counsellor: individually, as a couple, as a family (minus my daughter).

Hard stuff. But not nearly so hard as the admission I got from M after the counselling session.

As we sat in the park, waiting for the boys to finish up with our counsellor, he told me he had lied to me (again) last week about something I had asked. We were sitting on a park bench watching children in the playground. The sunny day turned cold and grey in a moment. Nausea. I looked at the nearest rubbish bin and began to calculate how many steps away it was.

Tonight, I stare at the ceiling. It is spinning. Who can I talk to about *this*? I'm sick with shame, shock, grief.

M's admission wasn't anything I'm obligated to report to the police, but it runs along similar lines. It brings me hurtling back in time to my phone call with my counsellor a couple days after his admission. Her first question to me after I explained the situation: 'Are your children safe?'

I can't process this. I'm living life on the edge of my worst nightmare. I'm able to talk to my sons as adults now. I know that other than a bad influence, poor monitoring, and perhaps spiritual contamination, my husband's addiction has not affected their sexuality. (In that he became an unstable and cruel person, it has very much affected their lives.)

But is my daughter safe? Now at seven? Will she be later: at 13 and 14?

I am covered in sweat and I can't stop the trembling. I am suspended between two levels of hell. One where I follow my instinct to flee, and my daughter grows up fatherless... 'just in case'. One where we stay and I am constantly vigilant of her safety. All day, every day. All night, every night.

I reach for a tissue and wipe my tears. Even if she arrives at adulthood, never directly victimised by her father, she will have to know sometime. There is no getting around the fact that her feminine identity will be rocked to its foundations sooner or later.

Trauma awaits her and I'm helpless to prevent it.

CHAPTER 4
Family Trauma

Some women find out about their husband's sexual addiction from their children. In that same moment, they may learn their children are being victimised. It's a mother's worst nightmare (outside, perhaps, of losing a child).

The only correct response in this situation is to remove the child/children from danger, immediately and then inform the authorities. Far too many families try to 'deal with this themselves.'

That is wrong at every level.

It sends the message to the offender that his offence should remain something hidden and private: that it's not *so* wrong. It tells the victim that she is, as she has begun to suspect, a rather low-value commodity – rather than a precious individual who deserves to be safeguarded. It also allows the perpetrator to wreak more havoc and destruction in the lives of children and families. Because no matter how much they say, 'I'll never do it again!' by the time the sex addiction has reached the level of sex offending, there's no escaping from it without long-term, professional and community help.

There are numerous reasons for the rise in child sexual abuse, both in and outside the Christian community. One reason is the sexualisation of children[48] and teens in media, and by the fashion industry. Another is the degradation of societal values around domestic violence, human trafficking, and healthy sexuality. Yet another is the lack of information in the general public (and sometimes among professionals) about sexual addiction. Finally, there is our unwillingness to talk about sexual matters: an unwillingness that creates dangerous levels of naivety. (See more in Chapter 18.)

The fire is also fed by the fact that there is so much shame around this form of sexual addiction. It is one of the most universally despised sins.

....

> Percentage of survey respondents who have conditions in their home around their husband spending time with children — 37%

....

From Man to Predator

No one starts off life as a pedophile, child pornographer or other type of sex offender.[49] Back 30 years ago, the road to this vile ending was a long one. As explained in Chapter 1, the sex addict is looking for the increasingly harder 'hit' of brain chemicals and he gets it by mixing the brain/body chemicals of arousal with those associated with fear, disgust, shock, etc. Thus, his brain craves these chemicals, but at the same time he is becoming increasingly unable to receive them (receptors begin to burn out on these super doses of neurochemicals).

Of course, finding materials involving children 30 years ago, to get the arousal/fear mix, wasn't that easy because western nations had laws for print media that made illicit materials of this nature hard to come by. Thus, it was harder to progress along the path. Not surprisingly, most child predators at that point were old men who had been walking the road for a life time: usually beginning as children or teens, when someone had sexually broken them.

Welcome to the new millennium where the internet has changed the game. In the last two decades there has been an explosion in free, child pornography available… and a simultaneous explosion in the number of children being victimised. Child pornography is one of the fastest growing types of businesses on the internet.[50] And today's viewer of child porn, possibly only a mere teen,[51] will be tomorrow's maker of it. The addiction, and the spirits that drive it, have an insatiable appetite for child sacrifice.

Addiction closes people off to experiencing peace and joy the way God intended. The brain chemicals associated with those sensations no longer release for the usual reasons: healthy interactions with people we love, intimacy with God, delight in the beauty of the world around us. In fact, these precious encounters become increasingly distasteful to the addict. Where we would see God and his beauty, they see God: a reminder of their sin and shame. The result is men who explode in violent anger at times against those who would, if they weren't addicts, make their lives more fulfilling. It also results in men running increasingly to their source of comfort: sexual arousal through the perverse… something more perverse than the last time, preferably.

Even if a man has not yet been caught up in the evil world of child pornography, it may just be a matter of time. It may not: his pathology may head other directions. However, any time we enable a man's porn, or other type of lesser sexual addiction, we are putting children at risk. Any time a sex addict enters recovery with his whole heart: the world becomes just a little bit safer for children.

....

I keep my children close. — survey respondent

....

A Child's Trauma

Children who have undergone the trauma of sexual abuse need protection, love, specialist counselling and community support. A book I recommend to comfort and help younger children (<12) is *I Can't Talk About It,* by Doris Sanford.

The time is long past for children in our churches, whom we know have been victimised, to be treated as lepers. Yes, they may be prickly, angry, hostile, withdrawn, exhibit poor sexual boundaries. They are wounded: that is how wounded people behave at times! Let's pray for grace… and pray for them![52]

Of course even if a child has *not* been molested by their sexually addicted parent, they will have been harmed by the addiction. Boys obviously have to overcome bad modelling. Even if they didn't witness Dad going into the strip club, or see his porn on the computer, they have almost undoubtedly witnessed some of the following behaviours:

- Inappropriate reactions to other women (sometimes including their friends) such as ogling, touching, and other signs of unhealthy boundaries
- Flirting with women
- Inappropriate sexual jokes
- Expressions of desire for other women

- Objectifying of women
- Unloving comments to their mother about her beauty, desirability, specialness
- Use of pornographic-leaning media (TV shows, movies, posters, calendars)

Those of us with non-Christian fathers often grew up with porn around the house: not particularly well hidden. M's father's porn was the starting place of his sexual addiction, something my father-in-law has recently apologised to him for.

Even if porn hadn't been in the picture though, simply seeing his mother dishonoured (through the other behaviours mentioned) would have damaged M's understanding of masculinity.[53] Thus M 'grew up' in body only and in turn, he damaged my sons' views of masculinity – something for which he has apologised. He's working to undo the damage now. The amendments go beyond 'giving up the porn'. They have meant working to become unstuck in his emotional and spiritual growth,[54] and working to honour them and myself.

My daughter, in particular, is reaping the benefits of this 'new and improved' dad.

> ...Objectification of women can be rooted in a girl's relationship with the first and foremost man in her life, namely, Daddy. Fathers, that is, can reinforce it by what they model to their daughters in their own reaction to women. What young girls see their fathers do matters more than what they hear their fathers say.
>
> — Dr Mary Andrews-Dalbey

The Effects on Girls

Like many girls of my generation, I grew up around porn. The first time I flipped through one of my dad's magazines, I was six years old. It damaged me, but fortunately in my later teen years, God delivered me from the worst of the effects, though residual influences haunt me to this day. Fortunately it is now illegal in most western world nations (including New Zealand and Australia) to purposely expose a child to pornography (a common luring technique of predators).

Even if a girl isn't overcoming exposure to dad's pornography (and many are viewing it online without dad's help), girls, like boys, also have to overcome his bad modelling. This includes modelling of immature, sexist behaviour, where it is obvious that Dad prefers:

- Women who flirt
- Women who dress in a highly sexualised manner (which the media is already telling her is essential)
- Women who make appearance more important than character
- Women who display poor boundaries with men
- Women who are surgically enhanced, and in other ways 'made up' to please men
- Women who are publicly venerated as objects/commodities: via the entertainment industry and/or mass media[55]
- Women who put their sexuality out into the public arena: via sexting, cybersex, stripping for the camera (phone, computer, etc.)

Bad modelling is the least of her problems, however, if Dad has brought his daughter directly into his addiction: either by molesting her or by luring her into some of the activities mentioned in the last point.[56] Please be aware that if this is the case, she will probably need long-term professional help for dealing with her trauma and shame. When Dad comes out in the open (whether or not it's because she has blown the whistle on him), she often ends up exposed and vulnerable.

In such a situation, we need to watch for signs of extreme distress in the victimised child/children for quite some time, and be ready to seek extra help for her/them.

Having our child offended against is such a heavy burden for a traumatised woman to carry. Why try to carry it alone?

Damaged Identity

It is difficult for people to understand just how powerfully a father's view of women, particularly his view of his wife, helps to shape a girl's feminine identity. If Dad isn't around, the media (who is always vying for the role anyway) will take over. If both are telling a girl that those of her gender are objects, whose value is determined by their appearance and willingness to be used, she is going to become emotionally and psychologically wounded. From there it's often a pretty quick downhill slide for her into degradation and pain unless God is in the picture to counteract the lies she has been led to believe (sometimes this happens even when God is, ostensibly, in the picture).

Dr Struthers puts the situation for girls bluntly: 'human beings are not a commodity. When forced to act as one, the emotional and psychological damage is severe.'

What lures women to believe the lie that her value is in her body? It's the quest for love. The most insidious message being sold to girls today is that male desire = love. Later in life, after allowing themselves to be used and discarded a good deal, our girls (now young women) usually come to understand this is a lie. At that point many decide that desire = power… and that will have to do. Thus the exploited become exploiters and round and round the dysfunction goes.

> Many clients have told me that they observed what kind of women their fathers were attracted to, and that's what they would strive to become. Unfortunately, these women were not talking about their mothers. — Dr Mary Andrews-Dalbey

Even When There is No Abuse

There's something in a child's heart that breaks when s/he comes to understand that mum is not loved and treasured by Dad the way s/he instinctively knows is right.

I can still recall many of my own moments of pain as I watched my father engage in some of the behaviours in the lists above. I also vividly recall the night, around age 12, I realised my dad was being unfaithful to my mother with another woman. My heart broke for my mother, and my whole idea of womanhood, marriage and intimacy began to crumble. Fortunately I had God to comfort me.

My daughter's turn to experience something like this is yet to come. I pray about it regularly. It's one of my key sorrows to this day. However, at her age, the most loving thing I can do for her is to preserve her innocence. (See 'Taking it Further' for more on age-appropriate disclosure.)

Anyone who works in the area of sexual addiction has had to witness the broken hearts of children and teens whose lives have been turned upside down by sex addicts. Issues include grief, loss, confusion, anger, as well as feelings of rejection and low self-esteem.

Sadly, I've seen some children side with their sex addict father, against mum. This is more common when mum's reaction to her husband's addiction has been to run off and have an affair of her own, or take up some addiction of her own. Both scenarios are all too common a phenomenon, as confirmed by the 2014/2015 Survey.[57] Let's remember, though, to be careful about adopting a judgemental/critical attitude when we hear stories of women doing things along these lines.

Frequently children are confused about how to relate to either parent following discovery of the addiction, especially if a separation or divorce results. When adult children choose to live with, or more actively work on the relationship with the SA parent, it can be quite devastating to the faithful parent.

In at least one case I'm aware of, because Dad's (known) 'indiscretions' with prostitutes were further in the past, and because this was a high-profile Christian family (and the children feared damaging the family's reputation and livelihood) the kids joined in the victimising of mum. The result? She ended up completely destitute and unsupported emotionally and financially for a time.

I was fortunate that my near-adult children did *not* blame me and supported my right to make the decision whether to stay or leave. They also showed a great deal of grace in the early days when the worst of my trauma was exhibiting itself and when the family was somewhat neglected due to the extra time required to seek help for myself. I am eternally grateful to them for that.

I was also blessed to see them enter into our search for information on sexual addiction. They learned a lot, confessed a lot and entered into the quest for purity with great zeal. God's redemptive work is marvellous beyond words.

Still, the betrayal of my children hurts me some days as much as or more than the betrayal to myself. I find it mind boggling that while I was pouring heart and soul (and love and breastmilk) into raising them to be healthy and whole people, my husband was undoing my work behind me. Intense pain for me: intense shame for him.

When Children Are at Risk

Any child whose world has been invaded by a parent's sexual addiction can benefit from specialist counselling. Please see the resources section at the end of the book for information.

In the meantime, if like me, you find yourself in some horrific no man's land: told your child has not been abused or in any way compromised, but feeling (rightly or wrongly) that there is still some future risk – or that what you've been told is a lie – you can acquaint yourself with the warning signs below and establish boundaries.

Understand as well that fear for our children's safety is a normal part of our trauma. As Dr Omar Minwalla, psychologist and director of The Institute for Sexual Health, writes: 'Sex addiction-induced trauma is a highly specific type of trauma that can include fear and panic of potential disease and contamination, fear of *child safety and potential of child molestation*, social isolation, embarrassment and shame and intense relational rupture and attachment injuries.'[58] [Emphasis mine.]

Once I had information that caused me to feel there might be some danger for my daughter, I set a new house rule that my husband was never to be alone with her: day or night. I know women who will have to enforce this rule until their daughters leave home. A man who is serious about recovery will respect this and bless his wife for her protection of her family (him as well as the kids).

If our husband (or anyone in our community) has a known history of child sexual abuse, or of seeking out and using child pornography, and he resists this boundary: we need to get away from him, preferably, permanently. No one with a history of molesting children, or any paedophilic tendencies should ever, ever have unsupervised access to a child of any age. Ever.

Sex offenders who are 'faking recovery' (many try this at some point) will always attempt to manoeuvre the situation back around to getting that access. However, we can take action. Please see the resources section at the back of this book, or search online for groups able to provide support.

Warning signs that a child may have been sexually abused

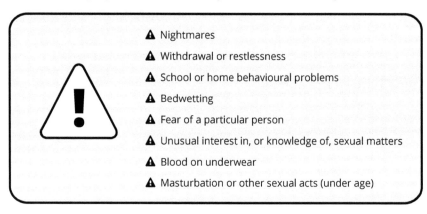

A Nightmares

A Withdrawal or restlessness

A School or home behavioural problems

A Bedwetting

A Fear of a particular person

A Unusual interest in, or knowledge of, sexual matters

A Blood on underwear

A Masturbation or other sexual acts (under age)

On the previous page is a list of indicators that a child may have been sexually abused. However, some sexually abused children show no visible signs, either physical or emotional, while being abused.

Let's remember that if we are made aware that a child – ours or someone else's – is being sexually abused, we have both a moral and legal responsibility to protect that child, and inform authorities.

I am aware that doing the right thing in such a situation is tremendously difficult and will result (in the short term) in tremendous pain, embarrassment and shame. One woman I am walking with has been blamed and harassed by numerous counsellors, members of the justice system, teachers, friends of the family and others. There have been days she has wondered if she did the right thing when she chose to report her husband as soon as she found out.

However, as the days have turned into months – and years – she has come to see that the overwhelming, short-term pain has brought long-term gain for her and her children.

Taking it Further

We need a plan when it comes to revealing information to our children. A controlled, personal explanation (not creating a Facebook post they may stumble across) is best: one that takes into account their age and ability to handle the information.

Very young children, obviously, should not be told anything about sexual addiction. On days when it is difficult to cope, they could be given a high-level explanation: 'mum is hurting in her heart', and reassurances that the child is loved and will be cared for.

Somewhat older children can be given a bit more depth. It may be appropriate to discuss how emotional pain sometimes causes us to behave differently than normal (with examples reflecting what they may be observing: crying, angry outbursts, arguments). End with reassurance that this is normal, will not last forever and that the child is loved.

According to Dr Stephanie Carnes, disclosure of the addiction is best left until at least age 15, unless there are concerns about the child's safety (in terms of abuse, their own sexual acting out, or uncontrolled disclosure by another party).[59] Optimal disclosure is best done by mum and dad together (assuming dad is in recovery), and details should be kept to what is age appropriate. Ideally, more emphasis should be put on the healing that's taken place than on the wounding that preceded it.

Other questions to consider: do I need help with childcare at the moment? Am I able to assess if there is any immediate risk to my children if I stay? If not, am I willing to reach out for help to professionals in the field who can help me evaluate our situation?

For Reflection: Psalm 27

Endnotes

48   Even non-addicts admit to struggling with pre-arousal/arousal around children dressed in a sexualised manner. There is probably nothing that causes a man, trying to do right, greater shame.

49   What follows is a discussion of one aspect of the development of the sex offender psychological profile. Please note that other, very complex and serious psychological and spiritual factors will be in play here.

50   Internet Watch Foundation, Annual Report 2008.

51   According to a study released in 2005 by the New Zealand Department of Internal Affairs, the largest group viewing child pornography in NZ was teens aged 15 to 19. A similar study conducted in Japan in 2007 by Malamuth and Pitpitan found that 23% of Japan's rapists are under 19: the highest demographic of rape victims are 13-19 year olds.

52   This is advice for adults. Children should not be made to befriend children with this kind of wounding. As adults it's up to us to be the strong ones who bear the brunt of others' anger and confusion — not our young children.

53   An excellent resource on the development of a healthy masculine identity is William Struthers' *Wired for Intimacy: How Pornography Hi-Jacks the Male Brain*.

54   One of his key resources has been the group study: *Living from the Heart Jesus Gave You*, Shepherd House.

55   Originally the preferred route for teen girls was the fashion or entertainment industries (including the Christian versions of these). A recent study by Media Smarts says, it is now the porn industry.

56   For an excellent parent/teen resource on teen sexuality and sexual brokenness in the modern world, see *Teen Sex* by Dr Patricia Weerakoon.

57   Of the respondents who said they had done something they regretted, 6% admitted they'd turned to addictive substances (most common: alcohol), 5% considered having an affair while another 3% admitted they did have an affair.

58   O Minwalla, 'A Call for Professional Action: Help for Partners of Sex Addicts', in *The National Psychologist*, June 2012.

59   S Carnes, IACSAS Redeeming Sexuality and Intimacy conference, 2015.

In the early dawn I lean across the bed and whisper.

'When I was a little girl, my father used to come down to my room to beat me. I remember standing on my bed holding my hands out in front of me and yelling, "No, no!".

He told me to shut up and close the curtains. I always had to close the curtains. These were beatings. He didn't want any of the neighbours to see and report him.

After he was done punching, slapping, banging my head against the wall, suspending me by my hair... whatever he was going to do that night, I would lie on my bed wailing.

As he left the room, my father would always turn and say, "Stop that noise or I'll really give you something to cry about."

So I would lie there, curled up in a terrified ball, trying to contain a tidal wave of pain. Trying to limit it to a trickle of silent tears.

Thinking about it now, I guess he just couldn't stand having a reminder of what he'd done.

When you tell me that you've lied to me because you're afraid of my reaction – that you might hear something you don't want to – are you so different than my dad?'

My husband looks at me, his eyes glistening. 'Not really.'

I meet his eyes, tears beginning to spill over. 'No, not really.'

CHAPTER 5

Toxic Lies

In Chapter 1 we looked at what ingredients make up the toxic stew that results in sexual addiction. Professionals have devoted much time and attention to trying to understand how sexual addiction comes about. Far less attention has been given to what toxic substances hinder a spouse's healing from infidelity trauma. It's important to recognise these substances early and take steps to protect ourselves from them. The most common toxins thrown at a woman during her trauma crisis are the lies:

- He isn't doing anything wrong
- It's your fault (at least partly)
- Ignore it: polite people don't talk about these sorts of things
- It's wrong to express your negative feelings to your husband

These lies are often expressed in statements such as those in the diagram below. Let's examine each of these ingredients in the toxic stew being fed wives of sex addicts.

Boys Will Be Boys?

Nate Larkin, in an address to a meeting of men and their sons, made a profound statement: children use women. Men love and protect them.[60] Nate is a former pastor; international author and speaker; and former user of women: i.e., sex addict.

What a challenge that statement is to society. We live in a world that glorifies immaturity… especially immaturity in males. More on how today's beer-drinking, game-playing, sports-watching, woman-using culture is feeding our sexual addiction epidemic will be dealt with in Chapter 18.

But beyond the 'blokes', who else feels that sexual addiction is acceptable?

A couple days after my husband's confession (the first of his series of confessions) as I was looking for help and advice, I stumbled across a forum where psychologists who also use natural medicine were discussing how to treat a newlywed who was looking for help with his habitual porn/masturbation habit. He wanted to stop because it was upsetting his wife. One of the professionals, a woman, glibly replied, '*she's* obviously the one who needs help, not him.' My response on reading this: a panic attack.

Even from a secular point of view, this statement is ignorant (and one of the men in the forum pointed that out to her). But as wives, it helps to be aware that we may encounter the lie that 'there's nothing wrong with what's he's doing'–even from professionals. Fortunately a growing number of counsellors and psychologists are becoming informed. Many are now in a place where they understand that any compulsive sexual behaviour that damages relationships is a problem.

At some point, however, we as Christians are going to come into disagreement with the secular world about what constitutes healthy, intimacy-promoting (Godly) sexuality and what is unhealthy, unethical (sinful) sexual behaviour.

Secular professionals will almost universally agree that illegal sexual activities are wrong and pathological. The majority will also take the stance that actually having intercourse with someone other than your spouse is ethically wrong (and if habitual, probably pathological). Anything before that line, however, they may consider 'grey' or even acceptable – especially if the act is not engaged in frequently enough to be categorised 'compulsive'.

In those grey and acceptable zones are such practices as masturbation with external media, cyber sex, hiring of sexual services outside of intercourse (or 'with intercourse' if the customer is single), flirting, fantasising (with or without masturbation), ogling/lusting (i.e. looking at female body parts for a hit of 'turn on' chemicals).

Overall, women[61] maintain a much higher standard for what we see as infidelity, as already discussed in Chapter 1. In his workshop at the 2014 IACSAS conference, Dr Struthers explained that men, with their more compartmentalised brain wiring, (as opposed to women's enmeshed brain wiring) are often likely to feel that unless *his* penis entered *her* vagina:[62] there was no infidelity.

Unlike other men, the God-man Jesus, was entirely clear about what constitutes the sin of marital infidelity. His words about it are recorded by Matthew in his gospel. I like Eugene Petersen's take on this teaching:

'You know the next commandment pretty well, too: "Don't go to bed with another's spouse." But don't think you've preserved your virtue simply by staying out of bed. Your heart can be corrupted by lust even quicker than your body. Those leering looks you think nobody notices – they also corrupt.' –Matthew 5:27-28 (The Message)

Since 'Christian' means 'little Christ' (i.e., follower of the teachings of Jesus), we'll find Christians calling men to a higher standard… right? Sadly, not always.

> I believed the lies that it was some how my fault, that I wasn't enough, that I needed to be skinnier, prettier or more sexual. — survey respondent on 'regrets'

You Aren't Enough

A Christian psychologist I know consulted me about a friend of hers who had discovered her husband's habit of hiring prostitutes. She said it was a very puzzling case because the couple had a good sex life.

I just shook my head at this. Though this woman was a Christian and a professional, she was sure the problem must lie with the wife – in her willingness to engage in sex with her husband or her desirability to him: the two main ingredients of a 'good sex life'.

Likewise, a woman I know was asked by someone in her church, after her husband had left her for his mistress: 'Did you do your wifely duty?' Though this brother was a blessing to her in many other ways, this question merely compounded her trauma and isolation. Yes, as a matter of fact, she'd been having sex with him regularly, even when it was absolutely repugnant to her to do so because she suspected infidelity.

One of the most painful accusations a traumatised spouse can hear is, 'His infidelity is your fault – you didn't do enough for him'. This is a lie. Always.

In Chapter 10 we will examine the lie that 'porn-star-experience' type sex will keep him from straying. Right now let's look at the 'you didn't put out enough' side of this lie.

Some Facts About Sex

The first thing we need to get straight is that sexual addiction is not about a man's biological need to have a regular orgasm. It's about an addiction to brain chemicals: the brain chemicals of sex mixed, as discussed in Chapter 1, with the brain chemicals of novelty, perversion, danger, etc.

There are sex addicts who can masturbate multiple times per day most days and still feel the desire for more. Some experts argue that men need an orgasm every 72 hours (this idea is increasingly being debunked); but you'd be hard pressed to find support for the argument that a man needs multiple orgasms per day. What's going on here is that the addict is soothing himself with a chemical high. This high damages the brain's ability to create/receive chemicals (particularly dopamine) that make a person feel happy and motivated. Thus, he needs more 'high' in order to avoid feeling depressed and unmotivated. See *Surfing for God* by Michael J Cusick for more on this.

> Sexual addiction isn't about sex. There isn't enough sex in the world to fill a hole that only God can fill. As a spouse, no matter how hard you try, you can't be God. The addict must assume responsibility for the choices made in sexual acting out. — Richard Blankenship

The 'Need' For Sex

As Dr Struthers points out in *Wired for Intimacy*, sex is not a 'survival need.' Survival needs include food, water and air. He writes, '…you cannot die from loneliness, celibacy or failing to join a social club.'[63] Since Struthers is adamant that masturbation is not a healthy (or godly) sexual practice, we can assume that by 'celibacy' he is talking about life without (self-directed) orgasm.

This belief flies in the face of much of modern psychology's current position on sexuality. It is, nevertheless, supported by both science and life experience. In the realm of science we know that a man has a 72-hour sperm production cycle. It takes 72 hours after an orgasm for a sexually active man to to reach maximum sperm capacity in his seminal vesicles. After that point, hormonal changes sensitise him to sexual stimuli,[64] i.e., he feels more motivated to find a release. If he does not find one (even during sleep), his body will begin to re-absorb what he has produced. This is how men can have a vasectomy and not 'explode'. The longer this man goes without an orgasm, the lower his testosterone levels drop and the less often he feels any physiological need to orgasm.[65]

That's why celibacy is possible. Why would we think God would make it biologically impossible when absolutely everyone is called to practice it at times in their adult life, such as pre-marriage, at times of illness, during physical separation? And that's not to mention during our periods.[66] I know numerous adult men and women who claim (and I believe them) that they are practicing full abstinence from sex. No, they don't even masturbate. Some of them did at one time, and they've given it up. Celibacy is absolutely possible.

Too many wives buy into the lie that their husband just needs more sex… then he'll stop. Thus, if they have to hop into bed multiple times per day (no matter how much their inner voice is screaming at them that this is wrong), they'll do it. If he wants a 'quickie'– though it rips her heart out, then sure. If it's been 72 hours, unless she's dead, she'd better perform.[67]

There are a number of men writing books and offering counselling in the field of sexual addiction who have supported the above scenario and others like it. Most of these men were sex addicts at one time themselves. I have noted recently, however, that the leading counsellors in the field (both former-addicts and non-addicts) focus more on marital intimacy than sex.

Still, many counsellors are tempted to take the recovery path 'of least resistance'. It's easier to tackle the acting out behaviours – i.e., giving up the hookers, the porn… maybe even the lusting (if you're *really* religious) – than false beliefs, past wounds and growth. If the former is the focus, more sex might be helpful. Then again, it might not be. An enormous number of sex addicts are impotent with their wives: shame, fear of intimacy, bonding to teenaged bodies, and the like playing a role there.

True healing, rather than addiction recovery, comes as the addict moves from 'child' (one who uses women) to 'man' (one who loves and protects). This is achieved through relationship with God, wife and others. We'll explore the topic of intimacy as a source of healing in Chapter 17. In the meantime, it's interesting to note that according to the 2014/2015 Survey of Wives of Sex Addicts, 72% of the women requested a period of abstinence at some point after disclosure. 42% found it had no particular effect on their marriage and 39% found it had a positive effect on their marriage.[68]

Thus, our husband's sexual addiction is not about how often we've been having sex (even if we stopped at some point). Nor is it about how 'hot' we are or what we look like. He would have done this to anyone he married. He would have done this no matter how much sex we gave.

Ignore It/Don't Talk About It

Many of us were brought up in families where sex was not a topic that was open for disucssion. Our church families have tended to follow suit.

Churches have long been notorious for hushing up talk of sexuality, particularly talk of the sexual struggles (and offending) of its members. This is as true today as ever, despite the fact that sexual topics are no longer considered taboo in Western society. Thus, while sex is the 'hot topic' everywhere from our primary schools to our radio stations, our churches remain mostly quiet on the subject – even though a survey conducted last year stated that 64% of Christian men are using pornography at least monthly.[69]

Says one survey respondent, 'Even though I had brought accusations that my husband was cheating on me, they [the church leaders] called him in once and that was the end of it. They allowed him to continue in lay ministry positions. He was able to bluff his way through without addressing any of his issues.'

A couple of years later, this woman's husband left the church. A few years after that, he was dead of HIV. Initially she was terrified she had been infected. Fortunately, she realised she *could* talk with others about her fears, and about her journey as a whole. In opening up, she found support and healing – outside of her church.

It was not until all of the life had been sucked out of me and I despaired of life that I was finally able to let go and realize 'I need to talk to someone!' I knew that if I did not get help I would die in my despair after 35 yrs of trying to fight the fight alone.

— Grace, friend and survey respondent

Co-Dependent?

Those women who choose to 'stuff' their emotions are the ones most likely to be labelled co-dependent. In a few instances, this label may apply.[70] However, one must not be too hasty about making judgements.

Though such a woman knows *something* about her husband's addiction, it's almost guaranteed to be only a portion of it. When she discovers one or two substantial 'somethings' (on top of those subtler clues that he easily explains away) he will lie, hide, cover up, etc.

She is then facing a painful ethical dilemma: one, that is in some ways, made more difficult by her faith. If she believes her husband (despite her instincts, despite the prompting of the Holy Spirit) she's being co-dependent – an enabler. Her life becomes one of constantly having to deny her instincts and, if the Holy Spirit really wants this topic discussed, even ignoring Him. If, on the other hand, she tells her husband she doesn't believe him (though she may have little, or even *no*, hard evidence), she is setting herself up for a battle extraordinaire.

A third option is available to her: spying and snooping for evidence. In the 2014/2015 Survey of Wives of Addicts numerous women mentioned that they regretted spying on their husbands. A couple of women explained that such behaviours did not help them feel more safe, but rather the contrary. These behaviours are also regularly labelled, 'co-dependent.'

Jason Martinkus tackles this issue in *Worthy of Her Trust*:

'… *There is a place for internet filtering and reporting, for GPS phone tracking, for following you around, for snooping through your email, for locking down the computer and the television and so forth. In the beginning of the restorative process, some of these are appropriate… some are necessary to give your wife a semblance of safety.'*

He adds that an even better way for the wife to regain a sense of security is for her husband to live transparently. In fact, more than transparently. He should become an 'active truth teller' who proactively offers information.

As for labelling a woman's spying/snooping behaviour 'co-dependent', Martinkus adds: *'Many recovery circles call this codependency or co-addiction. But I don't use these labels. While a "co-" state may be present to some degree, such labels can be applied usually only later in the process. In the beginning, it is too difficult to distinguish between self protection and codependency.'*[71]

Many sex addicts are master liars, manipulators, and abusers. It's hard to beat them at a game where they have all the information and we have almost none. Is a woman who isn't up to facing this kind of additional trauma, merely co-dependent? Is she co-dependent when she tries to get a leg up in the game by hunting out information? Reality is so much more complex than labels imply.

Just Get Over It

Many women have been told by their husbands: 'stop talking about your pain. It's stressing me out and then I'm more likely to start using porn (etc.) again.' Many recovery programmes for men support this idea. They state that if a woman shows her pain or anger then she is 'shaming' her husband. One programme I was involved in suggested a wife should punish herself for such behaviour. (More on programmes in Chapter 8.)

Addiction recovery is challenging. And the chaos that ensues when a man's addiction becomes known may not make his task feel easier. However, the idea that his recovery is more important than his wife (and her healing), his children, etc., is a very biased one. I liken it to a drunk driver running down a pedestrian. How obscene would it be for everyone to run to the aid of the driver to assist and console him, while yelling at the critically injured pedestrian to stop moaning because she was making the driver feel worse. Yet countless programmes operate this way.

One of the fundamental problems (we could even say, 'sins') underlying this addiction is self-centredness. Seeing himself and his pain as more important than his wife's pain, or the pain he's caused his children, may hasten his 'recovery' (i.e., not acting out); but it slows his deeper-level healing and the work God wants for the marriage. That deeper-level healing is what is going to keep him 'sober' long after he's done the intensives and the workbooks.

The Truth

Back in the 80's, I was given an absolutely dreadful pre-marital book to read by my pastor. In amongst the misogyny and the patronising attitudes, I found the odd gem. One of these was the statement that if the man were to do something so heinous as to betray his wife (who, on one hand, it suggested, was worth only as much as her chest measurement), he absolutely must allow her to bring up her pain and anger, whenever she needed to. However often she needed to. For as many years as she needed to. His job, as the perpetrator, was to take it. Gracefully.

Similarly, our Christian marriage counsellor, who we would visit within a of couple weeks of M's first disclosure, looked at him and said: 'You broke this marriage; it's your job to fix it.' She was calling him to a new level of manhood.

Taking it Further

Dr Sheri Keffer says, 'your marriage might be a casualty of sexual addiction. Your life doesn't have to be. Some of our partners don't understand how deeply they have been hurt. They're kind of just, "onward Christian soldier: I gotta keep marching into war."'[72] She goes on to say they need to put themselves on a gurney and let others help them heal.

Do you feel ready to reach out to safe people at this time? If not, what do you feel are the impediments?

> *For Reflection:* Psalm 116 and Lamentations 3:19-24

Endntoes

60 Pirate Monk podcast, episode 52, *Young Men and Fathers*, Feb. 17, 2011.

61 Perhaps I should say, 'older women'. A recent article out of Australia stated that 51% of younger women think that 'viewing some pornography is okay'.

62 In the case of heterosexual sexual addiction.

63 Struthers, ibid, p.156.

64 J Dobson, *What Wives Wish Their Husbands Knew About Women*, Tyndale Momentum, 1981.

65 H Hutchinson, MD, 'What are the Physical Effects of Sexual Abstinence?' Retrieved January 2015. <www.sharecare.com/health/sex-and-relationships/physical-effects-of-sexual-abstinence> Thanks to www.celibrate.org for the pointer.

66 Not only did God command that his people abstain from intercourse during the wife's menses, in traditional Jewish culture men are not to have any physical contact with their wives during this time: in case we were thinking they were obeying the letter of the law only.

67 Now that my marriage is in a healthier place, I keep the 72-hour information in mind: balanced with my understanding of how celibacy works. If you are dealing with someone who is fundamentally broken in their sexuality, you can probably file this information away for another day.

68 According to the same survey, 67% of wives who had requested a period of abstinence reported they had found it helpful to their personal healing.

69 Proven Men Ministry, 2014 survey results, as published at <www.provenmen.org/2014pornsurvey/christian-porn-stats/> Retreived, September 2015.

70 In more instances it is probably a case that she exhibits co-dependent traits.

71 J Martinkus, S Arterburn, *Worthy of Her Trust: What You Need to Do to Rebuild Sexual Integrity and Win Her Back*, ebook, page 37.

72 S Arterburn, *The Trauma of Sexual Betrayal*, April 27, 2014, New Life TV interview with Dr Sheri Keffer.

'What do you mean you didn't lie? You said you only used porn a couple times a year since we've been married.'

'I *didn't* lie. That's true. I only used porn about once every six months.'

'But now you've just said... once a month or so!'

'That wasn't porn, those were regular movies and TV shows.'

'What? If you used them to masturbate to, what difference does it make? It may as well have been porn. How do you figure you didn't lie when you told me "every six months"?'

M shrugs and averts his eyes. 'You only asked about porn.'

CHAPTER 6

Minimise, Rationalise, Justify, Blame

The level of shame that an addict has to live with is so high that he needs coping mechanisms in order to continue to look in the mirror each day. This is true for all addicts: alcoholics, drug addicts, sex addicts and others.

Counsellors working with addicts are particularly on the look out for the following four unhealthy coping mechanisms: minimising, rationalising, justifying and blaming. Addicts cannot grasp that they need help as long as they have these crutches to lean on. Thus, it is important that spouses learn to identify these false mental constructs. Even if they cannot change the addict's use of them, they can at least protect themselves from buying into the lies these generate.

Minimise

The great Christian scholar, GK Chesterton, once wrote, 'Men do not differ much about what things they will call evils; they differ enormously about what evils they will call excusable.' This is a beautiful description of minimising: the coping mechanism whereby the addict adjusts his perception of right and wrong in order to accommodate unethical behaviour and categorise it as 'excusable' or 'not so bad'. Minimising goes hand-in-hand with 'denial'. Addicts are minimising when they say things such as:

- It was just soft porn (or a strip club, a movie with a hot sex scene, a bit of flirting, fantasising, etc.)
- I don't have a problem: my friend Bert, he's in prison: now that's a guy with a problem
- I don't do it *that* often
- What I'm doing isn't hurting anyone
- I didn't have *intercourse* with the prostitute, that's a line I just wouldn't cross
- I don't use porn (I use regular, sexualised media and masturbate with that)
- I'm not addicted: I can stop any time

....

> In the beginning he minimised his use and did not understand my pain. As he took responsibility for his own behaviour and the effects, it became a more healing environment. — survey respondent

....

Rationalise

Rationalisers excuse bad behaviour (just prior to the behaviour) by over-intellectualising. Rationalising, like minimising, requires the addict to create a new moral code: one based on logic. Often there is a subtle shift here though, from what I'm doing 'isn't so bad' to 'it's actually good' or 'normal'. At times the new moral standard is a special one that applies only to the addict himself: for others the same action may be reprehensible. Some rationalisations one might hear from a sex addict prior to acting out include:

- I work hard, I deserve a little treat
- I'll learn how to please my wife better
- I have special needs others don't understand
- She (the prostitute) wants me
- She (my wife) can't expect me to stop everything at once

- There's nothing wrong with looking so long as… I don't touch (or, 'it isn't intercourse' or 'I don't get *too* rough', or 'she's 18ish').
- All men do this (also called 'normalisation')

> Boundaries I set: time out, [that is] no relating with my husband if he was communicating out of self pity, blaming, resentment, anger, rationalising, justifying or rage… — survey respondent

Justify

Justifying is similar to rationalising but is more dangerous, still. A rationaliser is grasping at straws in the heat of the moment. A justifier has coldly created a whole new moral infrastructure which supports his addiction. Thus, a justifier can argue quite calmly that he is choosing the best possible path in acting out… one that others should follow. In this way, he begins to put himself in the position of God: an act which can have horrific psychological and spiritual consequences. Some of the lines we might hear from a justifier are:

- Sowing our wild oats is an evolutionary instinct
- Monogamy is unnatural and oppressive
- What happens between consenting adults is no one else's business (not even their spouses)
- The _____ (violence, coercion, humiliation) is faked. Those girls have a great life
- This is about women's liberation and empowerment
- Freedom of expression is a fundamental human right
- I'm not religious, so I can ignore these draconian, religious ideas around sexuality
- I only use 'Christian erotica', 'ethical porn', or ' Christian[73] spouse-swapping'

> He always feels he is a victim and nothing is his fault.
> — survey respondent

Blame

Of all the coping techniques, 'blame' has the potential to be the most devastating to the spouse. While the wife is not the only person on the receiving end of her husband's blame stick, she will almost undoubtedly bare the brunt of it at some point if this is one of his coping mechanisms.

I am not trying to imply that every wife has always been the perfect marriage partner. That's not possible. However as Jason Martinkus explains, this is not the time (during the early days) for the husband to bring up the wife's issues.

'They (the men I counsel) cannot see their own issues because they are in denial and want to focus only on their wife's issues. This is just shifting the blame, much like what Adam did to Eve in the garden… Rather than deal with our own junk, it seems easier and less painful to focus on someone else's.[74]

Here are some of the lines one might hear from a wife 'blamer':

- My wife is too_____ (choose one or more: fat, flat, flabby, wrinkly, skinny, old, cold, boring, controlling).
- I love my wife, but she's just not my type, sexually
- My wife doesn't understand me or my needs (i.e., she won't support my desire for 'the porn star experience' or other perversions)
- My father set a bad example and got me started on porn
- My brother got me started on strip clubs when I was a teen
- If you hadn't gotten me upset, I wouldn't have acted out
- If you hadn't had those issues around sex, I wouldn't have had to go to prostitutes
- If you had ordered the pyjamas yourself, I wouldn't have acted out

Gaslighting

A more extreme and insidious blaming technique, one frequently embraced by sex addicts, is 'gaslighting'. This term is derived from the 1944 movie, *Gaslight*, starring Ingrid Bergman. In the film, Bergman's husband tries to convince her she is crazy using manipulative techniques. Some lines one might hear from a gaslighter are:

- I told you I was going to be coming home late tonight. You've been forgetting a lot of things lately.

- (When he begins driving recklessly.) There's nothing wrong with the way I'm driving. You're just imagining it.
- (When accused) You're crazy. I don't know what you're talking about.
- Why are you always so paranoid? Maybe you should look at getting some professional help.
- You're having a psychotic episode: you should go back on your meds
- The Holy Spirit told me to go hang out around the brothel. You just don't hear from the Spirit as well as I do. (This combines spiritualising with gaslighting.)

Gaslighting causes a woman to question her own intuition, her faculties, her ability to discern God's voice and even her sanity. These are of course, the God-given tools she needs to discover what is going on and protect herself and her children.

Every Man's Battle ministry founder, Steve Arterburn relates the story of how he ended up in a gaslighting situation. When his former wife told him, 'he was crazy and paranoid,' for thinking she'd had an affair, he challenged her saying,

'I want you to go on record. You would rather I believe that I'm crazy, I need heavy medication… I should go into an institution even – you would rather I believe all that about myself than you admit you made a mistake.'

Her response, like that of many sex addicts: 'Yes!' until the next day when she heard he'd scheduled a meeting with her affair partner.[75]

Thus Steve commiserates with wives who have had the gaslighting technique used on them. 'Every bit of survival instinct within you has been ripped to shreds by a man who wanted his addiction to survive.'[76]

Sadly, almost all the lines listed as bullets points in this chapter are ones I have heard, either personally or from women I was supporting.[77]

Ironically, those who use minimising, rationalising, justifying and blaming do so to escape their overwhelming shame and the fear of having their addiction exposed. Having to regularly face that level of shame and fear, would cause extreme psychological and emotional distress, to the point where action would have to be taken, if it weren't for a coping mechanism. So long as there's a lie they can grasp, addicts can continue on in the pattern that has become their prison. The truth, however, they will avoid at all costs. For more on the truth about sexual addiction and its effects on individuals and society, see Chapter 18.

Toward Healing

Pastor Chad Holtz counsels husbands on his blog, *Desire Mercy*, to 'tell her everything' and then 'tell her nothing'. By 'tell her nothing', he means:

'After you have confessed everything, offer no excuse. Do not attempt to rationalise what you have done, minimise it, or justify it.'[78]

May our husbands have ears to hear.

Taking it Further

We'll examine more closely what Pastor Holtz means by 'tell her everything and then tell her nothing' in Chapter 9 as we look more fully at the issue of disclosure. If disclosure is an issue in your marriage, you may wish to skip to that section now, or read Pastor Holtz's full article online. (See link at Beyond Betrayal.community.)

If Jesus was going to introduce you to some of his friends who had never met you, what would he say about you? Ask Him to help you make a list of the qualities he loves about you: that make you unique and special to Him. Review this list regularly, particularly when you are feeling ugly, unloved, rejected, etc.

I recommend this exercise for the addict in your life as well.

> ### For Reflection: Psalm 36

Endnotes

73 C Perez, 'These Christian Swingers Like Sharing Bible Verses, Sex Partners', *New York Post*, September 25, 2014.

74 Martinkus, ibid, p, 38.

75 S Arterburn, *The Trauma of Sexual Betrayal*, April 27, 2014, New Life TV interview with Dr Sheri Keffer.

76 Arterburn, ibid.

77 The three remaining lines come to me indirectly from my research.

78 C Holz, *Tell Her Everything Then Tell Her Nothing*, 2013, <https://desiremercy.wordpress.com/2013/10/27/tell-her-everything-then-tell-her-nothing/ > Retrieved, September 2014.

'Hello?'

'Mum. It's me'

'Lisa? It's... quarter after 3. What's going on?'

'I know. I'm so sorry to be calling at this hour... it's just
that I...' the phone slips from my shaking grasp and I
fumble, blinded by darkness and tears, to recover it.

'Lisa? Are you alright?'

The tears flow faster. 'Yeah. Well... no. Not really. M keeps telling me
more things... about his cheating on me. He told me tonight that he
used to fantasise regularly that I would die. He even fantasised that I
would die, and so would my best friend's husband – so that he could...
marry his wife. He wanted me to die so he could marry my best friend.'

The phone drops agains as I sink off my chair, onto
the floor. I am weeping uncontrollably.

A small, barely audible sound reaches me
from the direction of the receiver.

It's my mother, beginning to pray.

CHAPTER 7

Boundaries

Setting healthy boundaries is one of the key strategies we can adopt to protect ourselves and heal. Moreover, if our husband is at all interested in healing, our boundaries can also aide *him*.

Christian psychologists, Dr Henry Cloud and Dr John Townsend, literally wrote 'the book' on boundaries over twenty years ago. Their wisdom has helped change the lives of thousands of people. More recently they have applied that wisdom to specific relationships such as marriage and dating.

The duo describe boundaries in marriage as:

'...not about fixing, changing, or punishing your mate... It is more about taking ownership of your own life so that you are protected and you can love and protect your spouse without enabling or rescuing him or her.'[79]

Most wives of sex addicts, or men with sexual integrity issues, naturally begin applying protective boundaries during the initial crisis phase of their journey. We put emotional distance between ourself and our spouse, we consider consequences for the infidelity – especially if it should reoccur in the future.

Since our situation, as traumatised wives of sex addicts, is a serious one that requires swift action, consider that the doctors also say of boundaries, 'You need protective boundaries that you can put up when evil is present and can let down when the danger is over.'[80]

In Chapter 16 we will look more closely at how to know when the danger is over.

In this chapter we will focus on how to erect boundaries and use them well in the presence of evil.

....

> Above all else, guard your heart, for it is the wellspring of life. —Proverbs 4:23

....

Healthy Detachment

Detachment is about taking a step back from someone, and making ourselves less emotionally vulnerable in the relationship. In the 2014/2015 Survey, 83% of respondents said they had practiced detachment with their husbands. 77% of those said they had found it 'helpful' or 'very helpful' to their healing.

Beyond finding safety in emotional detachment, we also find space to focus on our own healing. The woman practicing healthy detachment frequently finds herself maturing, exploring her natural gifts and abilities, and exploring her relationship with God in new ways. This growth prepares us to be a better marriage partner or a more confident single. Thus, whatever the fate of our relationship with our husband, detachment puts us in a better position to move forward.

Emotional detachment is a healthy response to betrayal. There are, however, unhealthy ways people sometimes react when trust is damaged in their marriage. These unhealthy reactions include: complete withdrawal, over-investment in 'doing', addictions and compulsive behaviours, and one-sided relationships (usually where we become the 'giver').[81]

For myself, detaching left me feeling rather empty: until I learned to attach to our Abba (i.e. Father God). Over the course of time I found it helpful to take my feelings of emptiness, desire, longing and visualise presenting them to Him. This helped immensely. Once I began to re-attach with M, I didn't feel any desire to lessen my attachment to Him.

So was healthy detachment all that I needed to apply in my relationship with M? Sadly, no. As Dr Townsend says,

'…*There are times when the person's inner character is not what it should be, when the patterns are deeper and when the trust damage is more serious. These are situations in which appeals for the restoration of the relationship may go ignored, and conversations don't work. That is when you must draw boundaries – for your interests, for the sake of the relationship, and for helping the other person as well.*[82]

Setting Boundaries

Most women, in the early days after discovery (or after a relapse), feel they have lost all sense of safety. After seeking out our Abba and practicing emotional detachment with our husband, protective boundaries are the next best place to begin to regain that sense.

What exactly is a boundary and how do we set it? We'll look at specific boundaries set by wives of sex addicts in the next section. As for what they are, in general, and how they are set, Dr Townsend says:

'A boundary is simply a property line. It clarifies where you end and the other person begins. You form boundaries with your words, with your actions, and sometimes with the help of other people. Boundaries help you to be clear about what you are for and against and what you will and won't tolerate in your relationships.[83]

Far too many women feel they have no choice but to tolerate their husband's addiction/infidelity. This is not so. Not only has God given us the power to act, he expects us to do so, that we might continue to live in health and freedom. As Dr Townsend says,

'Boundaries help us to realise our freedom once again. Listen to the way that Paul tells the Galatians to set boundaries against any type of control and become free: "It was for freedom that Christ set us free; therefore keep standing firm and do not be subject again to a yoke of slavery" (Galatians 5:1 NASB).[84]

In other words, if our husband has manipulated us into supporting his sinful lifestyle: we are putting on a yoke of slavery from which Christ died to free us.

Now, our Father also wants to see his sons live in freedom. Thus, our motivation for boundaries should not be 'to control that man'. Let's let freedom, safety and love motivate us instead.

Now, truth be told, we may not be sure that we love our husband after we find out he's betrayed us. That's fair enough. However, we can still use our freedom to take positive action that will:

- Protect us
- Do him good
- Help our marriage

Protecting ourselves and doing something good for our husbands is not mutually exclusive. On the contrary: they often look very much the same. Of course, a man who is self-absorbed and has entitlement issues (hallmarks of the addict) may not see it that way originally.

However, our job is not to please our husband but to protect our children and ourselves. We also have a responsibility to love our husband – something different than having loving feelings for him or pleasing him. Loving means doing what is best for him – not necessarily what he wants in the moment.

> I am glad I did it [set boundaries], but it was the hardest thing I ever did. — survey respondent

Introducing Boundaries

Verbalising boundaries comes naturally to some women and seems like an impossibility to others. However with practice – and if needed, the support of others – any woman can learn how to create and communicate effective protective boundaries.

Some therapists feel that 'how' the boundary is verbalised is quite important. They fear that husbands will revolt if the approach is not right. As noted in Chapter 3, I believe that a man's sensitivity to the manner of communication is determined by such factors as culture, age, and maturity. His level of sensitivity certainly can be taken into account when explaining that a new boundary is being erected. That would be the most loving thing to do. If our husband is reluctant to embrace healing or boundaries, our communication style could help win him over (more on this below).

Of course, if we're angry – and it's okay if we are – we may not care much about his level of sensitivity. However, if we can take the high-road, let's do it: for ourselves (and our growth) as well as for the relationship. If necessary, we can walk away and come back and try communicating our boundary again another time when we're feeling less triggered.

Overall, though, 'how' the boundary is communicated appears to be a level of finesse beyond the scope of most of us. Of the women who responded to the 2014/2015 Survey, few were worried about how the boundary was communicated and far more indicated they were still trying to figure out what a healthy boundary is and how to follow through with consequences. Many still see themselves as helpless to set boundaries and they define the success of a boundary by whether or not their husband has changed. (More on this in the last section of this chapter.)

When asked what their regrets were around boundaries, 28% of respondents said they had no regrets about setting boundaries or about how they set them. However, 39% said they either regretted not setting enough, not being firm enough in setting/following up, or not setting them sooner.

··

> [Boundaries] helped me to gain clarity and to know what I can live with and what I can't live with. I regret that I was not more persistent in boundaries.
>
> — survey respondent

··

Specific Boundaries

According to the 2014/2015 Survey of Wives of Sex Addicts, the most common protection boundaries wives[85] set were around:

- Acting out behaviours/infidelity (cessation of) (66%)
- Attending counselling (64%)
- Sex (i.e., the couple's sex life) (56%)
- Media viewing (55%)
- Technology monitoring/filtering (55%)
- Travel (51%)
- Accountability (51%)
- Finances (50%)
- Time alone with children (33%)

Some of the protective boundaries set were specific to a woman's personal triggers. Common triggers are sexualised media, women who dress in a sexualised manner, sex shops, etc. Other, more specific triggers may be the people/places/objects/behaviours associated with our husbands' betrayal. Boundaries respondents set around their triggers ranged from the obvious 'no sex outside of the marriage' to such things as no flirting, visiting the beach, using the internet unmonitored, etc.

Sexual Boundaries

The subject of setting sexual boundaries is one I rarely find tackled in today's resources for wives of addicts. No wonder: this is one potentially divisive topic. 34% of respondents to the 2014/2015 Survey admitted that their husband's response to this request was very negative. Nevertheless, as already mentioned, 72% of the respondents requested abstinence anyway.

Considering that women's brains naturally connect sex and intimacy, this statistic is, perhaps, not so surprising. Moreover, some women have been used (even raped) by their addict husbands in the past and need time to process their pain around this.

Most women, if the marriage continues, will after a time, agree to have sex with their husband again. Some (particularly those who suffered abuse in the bedroom) will maintain a boundary around sex. In every case I'm aware of, the boundary isn't based on a desire to demean or control, but on the need to proceed slowly for the sake of rebuilding trust and a sense of safety. One boundary that I commonly hear: 'I (the wife) will always initiate sex going forward.'

Many of the survey respondents – who did not ask for sexual boundaries – admitted that they were motivated by the fear that if they didn't 'give him sex' he would act out. Thus, there are some betrayed wives who, even though they absolutely hate it,[86] have sex with their husbands regularly in the initial trauma crisis… at least for a time.

That's too bad, because 67% of the respondents who asked for a period of abstinence felt it had promoted their healing (only 8% felt it had been detrimental to their healing).

The husband who isn't overly fond of this particular boundary[87] would be well advised to work hard in other areas of the marriage to help his wife return to a sense of safety. The sooner she feels safe outside of the bedroom, the sooner she'll feel safe inside. As A Circle of Joy coach, and therapist, Louise Jewel says,

'The ingredients of a healthy marriage are: trust, transparency, communication, work and play, worship and healthy sex – in that order! Healthy and great sex is a reflection of all the other components of a great relationship.'[88]

As it so happens, some experts believe that a period of abstinence – generally three months – can help a sex-addicted brain to recover faster. So what we need may also be what he needs.

Accepting Boundaries

Some husbands are quick to embrace boundaries that protect their wives. A few even suggest them. According to the 2014/2015 Survey, respondents said their husbands were particularly quick to offer to put technology filtering into place. Thus the top boundaries adopted by couples (as opposed to just the boundaries wives asked for) were: attend counselling (81%), adopt technology filtering (77%), put limits on media viewing (71%) and cease acting out behaviours (71%).

M took himself off all media, calling movies and TV his 'gateway drug'. Five years later, he keeps this boundary in place. In this instance, M wanted the boundary for himself and his recovery, not for me. However, as it so happens, it works well for us both. Most healthy boundaries do.

But what happens when our husband rejects our boundary? Blankenship explains that most addicts will resist at least some boundaries. This does not mean the boundary is wrong: after all the purpose of the boundary is our safety, not the addict's comfort.[89]

> My husband's recovery was kick-started when my children and I moved out of the house. We believe that this interrupted his dissociation: reality caught up with him and forced him into action. — survey respondent

Boundary Resistance

Dr Townsend explains boundary resistance as follows:

'Remember that the boundary-resistant spouse feels that he should be able to do what he wants whenever he wants. With that as his operative principle in life, he will challenge and protest any boundary until he begins to grow up. Boundaries say that you cannot do what you want all the time.'[90]

Depending on the type of boundary, 22%-34% of wives reported encountering strong resistance[91] to it.

Means and Steffens emphasise, in *Your Sexually Addicted Spouse,* the need to explain to your spouse why you need the boundary. Jason Martinkus seconds this thought

– though he says this level of vulnerability can be reserved for the spouse who is resistant to boundaries requested in other ways. He calls this approach, 'appealing to the husband's protector instinct.'[92]

Townsend explains (and I agree) that women should state, in the same conversation, what the consequence will be for breaking the boundary. An example then of how the conversation with a boundary-resistant husband might run, is:

'When you ogle women, I feel rejected, unloved and fearful that you will act out again. If you do not refrain from ogling women when we are out, I have decided that I will leave immediately… in our car.'

By stating our boundaries in a way that makes it absolutely clear that our goal is protection, not control, we are offering our husbands a chance to rise to the occasion. Many of them are aware that they are the bad guy in the family. Many of them are dealing with the shame of having been failures as a husband. The ones who are serious about healing and saving the marriage will jump at a chance to be the hero for a change and make some restitution. (More on restitution in Chapter 16.)

However, in many cases he will not choose to rise. Then what?

Where we have direct power to enforce the boundary (e.g. 'no' to sex until after an STI test), we should stand firm. If there is an ongoing pattern of refusing to accept boundaries – and we've tried verbalising them with vulnerability – it's time to take action. This may include:

- Standing firm on those boundaries we are convinced are reasonable and healthy
- Following through on all stated consequences for all broken boundaries
- Arranging an intervention, i.e. having third parties (e.g., pastor, counsellor, family member, authors/researchers) join us in stating our boundary/ consequence and even helping us enact our consequence if necessary.[93]

Regarding this last point, bear in mind that many Christians do not understand how healthy boundaries work, and our husband may be able to find those to stand behind him in declaring our boundaries 'wrong' or 'unreasonable'. Sadly, enabling abusive behaviour is part of the Christian culture in some places. Remember that we have God-given freedom to make decisions for ourselves and determine what we will and won't accept.

If we choose to stand against unhealthy counsel, as well as our husband's sinful behaviour, let's remember that we are resisting people, not God. I have seen far too many women leave the church (I was one of them at one time) because they experienced abuse from the leaders for their boundaries and consequences. This is particularly true when the consequence was leaving.

The bible tells us God supports boundaries and consequences.[94]

'You were to Israel a forgiving God, though you punished their misdeeds.' – Psalm 99:8b

Let's not let anyone's lack of support for them deter us from creating protective boundaries and acting on them.

> Q: If you wanted to follow through on consequences
> for breaking boundaries/limits, what do you feel
> held you back?
> A: Finances

Consequences

Following through on consequences is difficult, as seen by the fact that only 15% of the 2014/2015 Survey respondents said they *always* followed through with consequences. However, another 37% said they *almost always* followed through.

There are a number of reasons why I believe many of us struggle with following through on our consequences. Some include:

- **Self-Doubt** Did we interpret the breach properly, or is our husband's perspective (because he always has a story) closer to the truth?
- **Guilt** – We know that we're not perfect. Do we have the right to enforce a high standard for our husband?
- **Fear** – Could include fear of retaliatory anger/violence, of being alone and unable to cope, or fear of financial consequences.

Also, some of us have been taught that our husband is our leader, our head. Do we have the right to hold him accountable for his actions, in that case?

For those of us who are struggling with the idea of consequences or with following through on them, a support group or counsellor can assist. Ideally they will help explain boundaries and consequences and hold us accountable for using them. They should also be available to encourage, and if need be, sit in on a meeting between us and our spouse.

Complying with our boundaries (and, setting his own), I believe, is one of the best ways a husband can make restitution to his wife for his betrayal. (More on this in Chapter 16.)

The saying 'the punishment should fit the crime,' obviously also applies to our consequences. When the crime is betrayal, we are already looking at a very serious offence. That said, some of the boundaries we set may not be about protecting us from his infidelity: they may involve other areas of his integrity that are harmful, but perhaps not quite at the same level (e.g., lying, irresponsibility).

The nature of the crime is not the only consideration in determining consequences. Other factors to consider are the frequency of the breach and the effects of the breach on others, such as our children. We will also have to discern what type of consequence is likely to make an impact on a man like our husband. As Dr Cloud and Dr Townsend say,

'Some spouses need severe consequences like separation. Others need less severe ones, like the following, to define important boundaries:

- *Cancelling a credit card*
- *Leaving for the party alone*
- *Ending an abusive conversation*
- *Refusing to bail someone out of a jam because of perpetual irresponsibility...*[95]

Obviously if our husband is slipping up in ways that breach our boundaries, we need to continue to keep a healthy emotional distance.

Many Christian women blanch at the word 'separation'. Bear in mind that 'walking away' (even just to the next room) is one of the few consequences we have complete control over. Numerous women in the 2014 /2015 Survey stated they regretted not separating sooner.[96]

Nate Larkin, founder of the Samson Society, states that 4 out of 5 sex addicts will not seriously engage recovery until their wife gives them an ultimatum.[97] My fear is that when women wait too long to leave, their husbands' chances of recovery go down. Moreover, our openness to a future reconciliation (should he heal and grow) commonly diminishes as the years go by and our pain reaches epic proportions.

That's because, at the end of the day, there's only so much healing a woman can find while her husband is stomping on her heart regularly.

> The prudent see danger and take refuge, but the simple keep going and suffer for it —Proverbs 27:12

Rules and Running

Rules – for the purpose of controlling behaviour, not just for protection – have their place in extreme situations. If a husband is already required to adhere to rules by the courts and other authorities, then his wife is ethically and legally required to help uphold these rules. Moreover, if he tries to contravene the rules: he needs to be reported to those same authorities. This is for the safety of everyone involved.

Though there needs to be room for compassion for everyone, we need to be as wise as serpents in situations such as this. With addicts who have – or whom we suspect have – adopted criminal behaviour or tendencies, we should be bold, firm and ready to act.

Marsha Means tells the story of Mary Miller – a woman who owned a copy of her first book for wives of sex addicts. Mary was strangled to death by her porn addict husband, (also a church deacon) who was seeking for a way to marry his mistress without scandal.[98]

We should never hesitate to flee a dangerous situation and report illegal behaviour. If we need help to take decisive action, we can call out to God and others.

> I had to set protective limits. His response let me know he had NO intention of giving up extramarital sex and pornography. My marriage ended. — survey respondent

The Limits of Boundaries

Sadly, it is still all too common for sex addicts to resist or break boundaries that would promote their wife's, and their own, healing.[99] Dr Townsend offers a thought on the subject of when boundaries don't seem to work, because our spouse disregards them, gets angry, or leaves us.

'…Boundaries aren't guaranteed to instil ownership, responsibility, or concern in someone. They can bring reality and clarity. They can protect you. They can show someone the path to change. But boundaries can't remove the other person's choice. So if you look at the real purpose of boundaries from this perspective, they do work.' [100]

Boundaries aren't about changing him or saving the marriage. They may very well have that effect, but it's not their main purpose. The goal of boundaries is to keep us safe and help us walk in that freedom Christ died to give us.

God sees us as his precious daughters. He has called us to refrain from putting on someone else's yoke (which is neither 'easy' or 'light'), but to be free.

Likewise, Jesus died to set our husbands free. As the Holy Spirit works to actualise this freedom in their lives, are we going to work with Him, or against Him?

Taking it Further

Do you feel able to ask for what you need in order to feel safe in your relationship/ your home? If not, consider finding a group or counsellor that will help support you as you make boundary requests.

When you make requests that push your husband out of his comfort zone, how does he react? Is that a positive sign or not? Are you able to stand firm?

Do your beliefs around biblical submission prevent you from requesting boundaries? If so, please read Chapter 10 for more on this.

Evaluate: How committed to his recovery and the restoration of your relationship does he seem to be? If he does not seem committed are you willing to start making alternate plans, or do you feel you would not be able to leave him, no matter what he did?

For Reflection: Proverbs 4:23, Proverbs 27:17 and Ezekiel 13:22

Endnotes

79   H Cloud and J Townsend, *Boundaries in Marriage*,
      Zondervan, 2002, ebook, p. 25.

80   Cloud and Townsend, ibid, p 53.

81   J Townsend, *Beyond Boundaries*, ebook, pp 30-31.

82   Townsend, ibid, p. 47.

83   Townsend, ibid, pp. 33-34.

84   ….

85   These results comprise only those boundaries wives requested. In many cases
      the husband also offered to adhere to boundaries, before he was asked.

86   Many survey respondents listed 'not setting sexual boundaries' as a regret.

87   27% of respondents said their husband initiated a period of
      abstinence. This may be related to issues of intimacy aversion.

88   L Jewell, retrieved August, 2014 <http://
      louisejewellcounselling.blogspot.com>.

89   R Blankenship, ibid, p.119.

90   Cloud and Townsend, ibid, p. 406.

91   L Taylor, M Means, '2014/2015 Survey of Wives of Sex Addicts.'

92   J Martinkus, *Gaining Back Trust*, New Life TV, November 13, 2014.

93   For an outline of how to run a scripturally based intervention with a husband
      who is resisting boundaries around either acting out or seeking help, see:
      http://www.pureintimacy.org/w/what-to-do-when-a-spouse-refuses-help/

94   'Are Boundaries Biblical?', retrieved December 2014 <http://
      www.gotquestions.org/boundaries-biblical.html> .

95   Cloud and Townsend, ibid, p. 75.

96   14% of women said they regretted not putting in more boundaries, 14% said they regretted not being firmer in sticking to boundaries and 10% said they regretted not establishing boundaries sooner. In a different question, 7% of respondents stated one of their biggest regrets was not ending the relationship sooner.

97   N Larkin, IACSAS Redeeming Sexuality and Intimacy conference, 2015.

98   M Means, IACSAS Redeeming Sexuality and Intimacy conference, 2014.

99   According to the 2014/2015 Survey of Wives of Sex Addicts, the boundary that most frequently got a positive response from husbands was technology filtering. The highest number of negative responses (by husbands) were for boundaries around sex: the couple's marital sex, and the addict's acting out.

100   Townsend, ibid, p. 39.

'Hi, my name is Lisa and I am the partner of a recovering sex addict and intimacy anorexic. I am healing from...'

I scan the list on the sheet in front of me:

Co-sex addiction... nope.

Mothering... huh? Nope.

Spending/shopping... no money, so no worries there.

Codependency... nope.

Depression... mmm, maybe. Still too much in shock though.

Control... nope.

Anger... not so much this week.

Avoiding... no.

Escaping... no.

Food Addiction... ha, ha... I wish. I can still barely eat.

Low self-esteem... bingo.

'I'm healing from low self-esteem.' I look around the table at the four other attendees of the meeting. Directly across the table I see a sad, sympathetic smile and return it before looking back at the book and reading:

'My acting behaviours have been...'

I quickly scan the huge list of dysfunctional behaviours, shaking my head frequently. Then my eyes light on one. 'Negative self-talk!'

I move to the next paragraph. 'My consequences for doing the acting behaviours were...'

I look up at S, the co-ordinator. 'Sorry I just got this book today, so I didn't have any consequences for myself this week. What does that mean anyway?'

S smiles warmly. 'Consequences are punishments you choose for your acting behaviours. Consequences help train you out of doing them.'

'Oh. So... what types of consequences would you normally choose for something like negative self-talk?'

S holds up her wrist. 'Well one of our favourites is wearing the elastic band. Every time you catch yourself saying something negative to or about yourself, you just pull it back and snap it.' I notice she looks a little uncomfortable.

I nod. Deep inside, something feels wrong. These guys are the experts though... and I don't have enough life left in me to question.

CHAPTER 8

The Company of Suffering Sisters

Where the 'co-addict' view of wives of sex addicts prevails, women are generally encouraged to attend some form of 12-step programme. After all, we've got an 'addiction' to kick (or at least co-dependent behaviours).

Even if we decide not to operate out of the co-addict/co-dependent model, there is still a place on this journey for support from those who have 'been there'. Meeting regularly with even one other woman who has lived through this trauma and come out the other side, can be enormously uplifting.

Before our family immigrated, I would spend six weeks at the partners' support group described on the previous page. Despite the ridiculous rules-based workbook (particularly ridiculous as not a single woman there exhibited co-dependent traits to a strong degree), this group was an enormous blessing to me. The women were hurting, loving, real and altogether amazing. This was one of my first experiences of being completely vulnerable with other women, and having them be completely vulnerable with me. I was very sad to lose them, but was hopeful that I would find a similar (maybe even better?) support group waiting for me in the southern hemisphere.

As it turned out: there was. But only because of Skype. The next and better group would be based overseas. Sadly, I found that a phone group doesn't allow for the level of bonding I experienced with my first group. I gained some and lost some once we moved.

12-Step Groups

Most of the 12-step programmes for spouses of sex addicts are based on 'the religious approach'. I am using 'religious' in its most negative sense. The groups are rules-based, performance-oriented, and punitive. Jesus came to show us that religion just weighs us down… relationship with God is where we will find life and healing. Once we have life and healing, we naturally follow God's rules.

The first support group I attended was not, strictly speaking, a 12-step group; nevertheless, it followed that model to a large degree. The main problem with the book/workbook we were going through was that the author believes:

- Wives of sex addicts are all co-dependent
- The husband's recovery is paramount, and wives are undermining that with their negative behaviours
- Wives should use self-punishment to train themselves out of those behaviours

Instead of accepting our trauma reactions as normal, and encouraging us to find healing from our trauma (which would help move us past the 'undesirable behaviours'), this expert[101] told us we needed to be punished for these reactions.

Thus, not only are some wives being blamed by their husbands (for his acting out or for her 'overreacting' to it), and by therapists using the older treatment model – they may even find themselves being blamed at their 'support' group. Women are constantly being told to shut off their intuition, shut down their emotions, and in general: shut up and 'get over themselves.'

I do have codependency issues, yet… it took a diagnosis of PTSD and addressing those issues first to begin the healing process. The co-addict model sent me deeper into depression and I never felt like anyone could see or understand I genuinely wasn't trying to control my husband, nor was I being judgemental and trying to make him pay, I was simply TERRIFIED and I needed comfort and reassurance… The co-addict model kept saying, 'pick your own self up by your bootstraps and get over it. Get over yourself!' I couldn't figure out how to pick myself up, nor could I find my bootstraps. And how do you begin to 'get over' a catastrophe that you supposedly helped to create and are now suffering the consequences of. It was more than I could bear…'

— survey respondent who spent 7 years in a 12-step group before moving to a trauma model group

Sadly a quick search on the internet reveals the stories of women who, after being beaten up by support group leaders accept the blame being thrust on them. In one story a woman related how her husband cheated on her and lied about it *again*. Her 12-step programme group leaders, in a discussion with her and her husband, told her she had no right to be angry. Didn't she understand that this was the way it was going to be in early recovery? She was then told she needed to go talk to God about her unforgiveness issues (more on forgiveness in Chapter 15) because this was at the heart of her marital problems.

This is spiritual abuse, and sadly this woman became victimised because she accepted what her facilitators were saying as the truth. No doubt God does want to walk this woman through the process of forgiveness at some point. But at this crisis moment, He wanted to minister to her grief and trauma. Sadly there was no one willing to work with Him.

If a woman isn't 'crazy' with shame and pain before trying to find help, she certainly will be after she's had other layers of guilt and trauma (such as this) added to her existing load. Thus, if we find ourself in a support group with leaders who operate in this vein, the best thing we can do is leave. There is better support out there for us.

If we find a group more like my own: one with misguided resources but loving sisters, remember, it's okay to be there for the fellowship and whatever learning we are able to discern (prayerfully and intuitively) as right. And, let's not be afraid to suggest (as H did in my first group) that perhaps the group should explore some other types of materials, such as some of those we will discuss next. Though my first group did not make the switch, the group discussion we had about other options prompted me to seek out materials based on the trauma model.

Trauma-Based Approach

Eight months after moving from 'up there' to 'down here' I would find another support group. By that time I had finished reading *Your Sexually Addicted Spouse* and was on the look out for resources from the same authors. With a bit of googling I found the website for *A Circle of Joy* (ACOJ) ministries.

ACOJ, Marsha Means' ministry to wives of sex addicts, offers partners of addicts (and the addicts themselves) many levels of support. At the time of writing, that support includes a one-time, free 60 minute call to a coach, a free newsletter, a closed, online forum (for a nominal monthly fee) and various twelve-week groups. It was the entry-level group that I joined. And while I did not connect with the women as easily as I had in the face-to-face group, I received an immense amount of encouragement and assistance toward healing and growth. Moreover, I would get my first glimpse at how uplifting it could be to help other women who were in their discovery crisis days.

After the entry group, I would move on to a second ACOJ group where we studied the *Life Model*: a book, from US-based Shepherd House, on emotional growth and trauma recovery. All the adults/teens in my house found this an interesting read that challenged us in many positive ways.

As of the time of writing there a number of other groups available, including:

- 'Journey to Healing and Joy' for women whose husbands struggle with same-sex addiction
- 'Crisis of Faith', for those whose trust in God has been damaged by their journey
- 'Boundaries in Marriage to A Sex Addict'
- 'Learning to Trust Again'

Shelley Martinkus, of Redemptive Living for Women (US), also runs support groups for wives, with the help of several additional coaches. Shelley is the author of the *Rescued* workbook for wives of addicts, a speaker and the co-star of the Kitchen Convo series, which I quote frequently in this book. See the resources page for more information on Shelley and Redemptive Living.

In the UK, therapist Paula Hall (paulahaul.co.uk) offers support groups for both addicts and partners. While her workbooks and other resources are not Christian, per se, her approach is, nevertheless, very partner sensitive.

> Only once did I attend a 12-step group. I did not return, as they were quick to use the label co-dependent (which I was not) and were quick to advise divorce, as they believed there was no healing. I did not return. I have since started my own mini group with two other women. — survey respondent

Counselling

There are many therapists who offer counselling to wives of sex addicts. Most of these do not have specialist knowledge of the partner-trauma model. This is particularly true in our part of the world where the co-dependent model is still popular.

I believe that the ideal therapist for the betrayed wife:

- Doesn't universally work from the co-dependent model
- Has specialist training in sex addiction and partner trauma
- Has 'been there'

As of the time of writing, IACSAS is scheduled to run a certification course in New Zealand. The result, I hope, will be an explosion in the number of profesional therapists, in Australia and New Zealand, trained and certified in the best practices of sex addiction recovery and partner-trauma healing. I plan to keep a list of certified therapists at www.beyondbetrayal.community.

Coaching

There are also now a number of non-therapist coaches[102] who have dedicated time and energy to walking alongside betrayed wives. While initially we might think that we can get all we need from a good therapist (assuming we can find one), the coach, nevertheless has many unique gifts to offer us.

I admit to a certain bias here as I work as a coach. When I spoke to my mother (an addictions counsellor of 30 years) about the possibility of becoming a therapist, she told me not to underestimate the help of lay people. She added:

'Therapists have limitations placed on them. We can't share our personal stories, for example, or others' stories. People benefit from connecting with those who can share their stories including their pain, weaknesses and vulnerabilities.'

While the number of private coaches is still small, there is a growing body of them, particularly in the US, who will work one-on-one with women based in other countries over Skype or the phone. Please note that some coaches charge money as they have quit jobs in order to be supporting women full time. Others, like myself, limit the number of women we support, but don't charge a fee.

There are so many women left destitute by their addict/unfaithful husbands that I encourage you, if you would like to work with a coach and have the resources to do so, to hire one. If you have the option, leave the free coaching for those who need it most. Alternatively, if you have the resources and a free coach is all you can find, consider donating to an organisation, such as APSATS, IACSAS or A Circle of Joy ministries, that is working hard at the international level to support those ministering to wives of addicts.

Connecting is Worth It

I must admit that I drove to my first support group meeting with low expectations. It was my therapist who talked me into going. I was in 'isolate' mode. I withdraw in painful circumstances and the idea of being with women in particular – who would by virtue of their gender remind me of how 'deficient' I was in my husband's eyes – seemed impossible. I'd already read numerous books on sex addiction, so surely there was nothing new I could learn from these women!

I've quite possibly never been 'more wrong' in my life.

What I gained from this group was, not so much knowledge, though there was that too (predominantly gleaned from the women's stories), but a place to grieve, and while grieving, have the empathy of others wash over my parched soul. In the safety of that place, my heart cracked open ever so slightly, and I was able to show myself – beat up, bruised and bleeding – and collapse into the embrace of other wounded sisters.

God bless them – and all those who reach out in love to the hurting.

> To have a hope of an intimate, healthy relationship in the future, you have to clean up the emotional wounds from the difficult relationship in your past. You don't need to talk about every detail of what happened, but if the relationship was important to you, you simply must talk about it with a few safe people for some period of time. —Dr John Townsend

Finding a Support Group

Finding a good support group is not always easy. According to the 2014/2015 Survey of Wives of Sex Addicts, only 36% of respondents from Australia had ever attended a group, as opposed to 55% of respondents worldwide. Of those in Australia who had been in a group, 2/3 had joined one which used materials from the 12-step model. Not surprisingly, they reported low satisfaction with their group.

Those who had made use of the online A Circle of Joy groups, however, reported higher satisfaction with the support received. Nevertheless, perhaps it's time that more face-to-face groups for spouses of sex addicts became available in Australia and New Zealand. I am aware of groups in Queensland as well as in Auckland, the Christchurch area and the Northland (of New Zealand). If you feel this is something Father God might be calling you into, see the resources section at the back of the book.

Taking it Further

Many of us have a tendency to isolate ourselves when we are in pain. This may be a wise option for a short time, but ultimately it is not what is best for us. If you have not yet sought out a support group, coach or counsellor, what factors do you think have kept you from doing so?

If you are currently getting some support, is there more yet you should be seeking out? Are you getting face-to-face support? Are you getting lay (e.g., coaching or group) support as well as professional? Are you getting family support? Are you getting specialist support that validates your pain, as opposed to blaming you for your situation? The larger the variety of support, the easier it is to get quality results.

A number of support materials were listed in this chapter. You will also find a resources section at the back of this book. Will you consider making time in the next week to look into some of them?

If you have been on this journey some time and would like to start your own local group, but need help doing so, see the resources section at the end of this book.

For Reflection: Ecclesiastes 4:9-12

Endntoes

101   And while I do not feel this man, who makes his living off of counselling SAs and their spouses, and selling books, is on the right track in this one regard: his work, research and many of his teachings are not wholly without merit.

102   The term 'coach' may refer to someone who has taken a coaching programme and is accredited, or simply an experienced mentor who works with people looking to move beyond a difficult situation. Some therapists are also accredited coaches.

The prairie sky is split in two. A nano-second later, a crack of thunder rocks our otherwise stationary car.

I sit motionless: stunned. Stunned by this terrifying thunderstorm, stunned by what has just happened in the town a few kilometres behind us. Stunned that my always 'together' husband has pulled the car off the road and is sobbing with abandon into his hands.

It had been his idea: the polygraph test. He'd heard about it from his recovery counsellor and volunteered. I'd agreed. Admittedly, I had some questions I wanted answered. Every week since his first admission, there has been more – more stories of betrayal, more 'corrections' to the original story, more about the frequency of the betrayals and the nature of them... more nightmares to process.

But when he'd made the appointment with a forensic polygraph technician, he'd assured me I knew it all now. He had come completely clean and was going to prove it. His counsellor had said it would be a starting place to rebuild trust.

There had been one particular question burning in me: 'is my daughter safe'. I'd made sure the question pertaining to her (actually to children in general) was put front and centre.

After the test, the technician came out of the room and told me M had passed on that question. But before I could breathe my sigh of relief, I was told he'd failed on a later question.

I haven't spoken since and even now feel too numb to speak. I turn to M. I have never seen him so broken. Is it because of the blow he's dealt me again: the unexpected scorpion in place of the egg?

No, the words he mumbles over and over again: 'I've never been so humiliated in my life. He treated me like a criminal.'

CHAPTER 9

The Last to Go

Pathological lying is part of the profile of any addict. Within the first few days of M coming out about his pornography use, my mother (the addictions counsellor) warned me: 'the lying is the last to go'.

Some addicts, she warned me, never let go of it. They build up a fantasy world for themselves, where they are the hero. The reality of who they are and what they have done keeps pushing them back into their own delusions, until they actually believe the stories they've concocted.

I have had to repeat this explanation to many women in the last few years. Yesterday, it was N, wife of a sex offender who told his parole officer that his victim (and daughter) was a liar who had made the whole thing up. The parole officer was so shocked by his inability to accept responsibility for anything he'd done (despite having plead guilty to all the charges) that she called N and warned her that her husband is extremely dangerous.

She's right. Liars are dangerous and trying to live with a pathological one can be terrifying. This is particularly the case when we get to the point where we ourselves are having difficulty distinguishing God's truth from their lies. (See Gaslighting, Chapter 6.)

In the early days of the failed lie detector test – meant to rebuild trust – I felt panicky most of the time. I cried out continually to God to be my safety. The trouble was, in my hyper-vigilant state, it was very difficult for me to hear God's voice on this or almost any other issue. This would continue for many months.

> He lies about everything — daily/pathological.
>
> — survey respondent

Why Do They Have to Lie?

In his book, *Stop Sex Addiction*, Dr Milton Magness, puts forth some theories about why so many addicts lie – even about small things. He points out that lying becomes a survival skill, or means of attention, for many children: one which does not automatically disappear in adulthood. In any situation where the habitual liar feels even mildly threatened (even with their wife's disappointment or criticism) he/she will turn to the familiar refuge, sometimes without even planning to do so.[103]

It may work for awhile, but the pathological liar is bound to get caught from time to time. Each instance erodes a partner's trust. If the liar is a known sex addict as well, then he's likely going to move from 'ground zero', as far as trust goes, into the trust 'minuses'. And for good reason: he has lost all credibility by living a double life. Every lie just adds further insult to devastating injury.

In the 2014/2015 Survey of Wives of Sex Addicts, 'Broken trust' was listed as the number two reason for the failure of the marriage, just after 'his sexual addiction/ sexual integrity issues.'[104]

> We are currently back in couple's counselling and I am somewhat hopeful, yet a lot depends on the polygraph.
>
> — survey respondent

What We Learn from Polygraphs

Though very popular in certain US addictions counselling circles, the polygraph method of rebuilding trust has, in fact, proven to be a bit shaky.

Therapist Joan Condie states,

'The validity of polygraph testing has been debated for years by researchers and respected counsellors. The courts refuse to consider the test results as reliable for proving innocence or guilt. The fear of being caught could result in a quicker confession, however, problems occur when your marriage is at stake and you get a false positive or a false negative

reading. Also, consider the possibility of gaining a sense of security, but he then has another affair or seeks out porn again immediately following the test. How many polygraphs are enough? If you feel you need test results, your marital problems are more severe than you might realise.[105]

That said, I would consider a man's adamant refusal to take a polygraph test (when the idea is introduced to him) as suspect: unless he is aware that the results are not necessarily accurate. However, this is not, at present, a well-known fact.

In my case, M kept offering to do the tests. Starting six months after we arrived down under, he would try again. In total he failed three polygraphs on the topic of his disclosure. In every instance he was devastated and declared adamantly that he had confessed all he could think to: with the caveat that his memory is not good in general, which is true enough. We have met one other man with a similar story. This husband, however, did pass his second polygraph (which asked the same questions as his first, failed test).

Though M did not stop lying over night (mostly about his day-to-day struggles with lust), there have, in fact, been only two new confessions related to his disclosure from the day of the first polygraph to today (over five years later). Neither were particularly earth shaking and I choose to believe that he had originally forgotten these incidents.

As for why the ever-popular polygraph didn't give us the results he expected, M insists that even hearing the questions (when he knows 'this time it counts') makes him start to panic.

Of course, I may just be gullible. I am taking the word of a known liar over that of an impartial machine. The thought has cost me my sleep many a night.

Uncovering the Truth

Part of our trauma lies in the fear of future betrayal. Additional disclosures have a similar effect: each piece of information has to be processed as if it has just happened. Thus, we should give out trust judiciously to a known liar.

Still, how do we continue in a relationship where there is no trust? This question is especially pertinent when he is found out, not through admission, but through 'being caught at it' (75% of cases says one study).[106] How do we trust when we were told we had the whole story and then within a few days find there's more... and then more?

Fear of having our hearts crushed, again, has motivated many of us to play the detective. Very few women want to descend to spying, but many feel they have no choice considering what's at stake. In the online 2014/2015 Survey of Wives of Sex Addicts, 9% of the women who were willing to volunteer their dearest regrets on this journey listed 'spying' as one of them. As one woman aptly put the results of spying: 'I have more details than I needed to see/hear, [details] that I can never forget.'

Marsha Means counters with the idea that using spy technology could reveal a truth that might save a woman or child from serious harm or even death.[107] This is doubtless true in some instances. However, we probably don't want to play detective for the rest of our lives. Perhaps where there are ongoing lies, acting out, bullying/abuse and resistance to becoming transparent, it would be best to put in some very firm consequences for this behavior – even separating. There is no better 'first step' to physical safety than physical space.

> The major impediment to healing for me has been… the secrecy/lying about it [his acting out] and the partial disclosures. It seems that whenever I have gotten myself back on my feet, [and] started to trust again BOOM! I am knocked down. — survey respondent

Disclosure

So if polygraphs and spying don't necessarily make us safer, what will?

The first step a man needs to take, in order to re-establish himself as a safe person to be in relationship with, is full disclosure. Disclosure refers to the process of giving one's wife all the details about the sexual addiction and betrayals.

All the details?

All the details. The wife should make the decision about what level of detail is too much or too little. She, after all, is the one who has been offended against. She is the one who has to forgive, and some of us, really want to know what it is we're being asked to forgive. I have a very fertile imagination. Left with a void, it will always fill in the blanks with something far worse than actually transpired.

Unfortunately some SA counsellors encourage men to withhold information from their partners, or at least some of the details. This is not sound advice and encourages the pathology the addict tends toward naturally, i.e., lying and self-protection. It is also very condescending behaviour to the spouse: suggesting she doesn't actually know what's best for her. The vast majority of women have a very good sense of what's 'too much information' and should be allowed to speak for themselves on this.

Remember that saying from Pastor Chad Holz (Chapter 6)? It was, 'tell her everything, then tell her nothing.'

Let's look a little closer at how that would apply to disclosure. Holz explains to husbands:

'When you are involved in sexual sin, whether online or otherwise, you are both desecrating the temple in which God dwells (your body) and depriving your spouse of a right that belongs solely to him or her. So yes, you must tell your spouse, and you must tell her everything.'[108]

He adds that disclosure needs to take place all at once. Information must not be dribbled out over time.

Good advice, because as many of us know, this approach is much more painful than having everything revealed at once. And, as mentioned above, withholding information initially, damages trust more than getting the full story in one sitting.

But what does Holz mean by, 'tell her nothing'? This refers to excuses a man might be tempted to make for his behaviour.

'After you have confessed everything, offer no excuse. Do not attempt to rationalise what you have done, minimise it, or justify it. You have basically three responses from now on: I'm so very sorry, and, You're right, and, I love you.'[109]

Shattered Trust

Means and Steffens explain trust building this way: 'Trust is shattered when sexual betrayal and relational trauma occur… The hard truth about trust is that it must be earned before it can be given, especially after a sexual violation.'[110]

In *Worthy of Her Trust*, Jason Martinkus lists nine 'non-negotiables' of trust building. His top three are spiritual commitment, honesty, and transparency in the big and little things.

I found Martinkus' thoughts on transparency, in particular, a breath of fresh air.

Martinkus calls men to go beyond honesty to transparency. This means not only laying open their private life and actions to their wife, but actually inviting her to come in and take a look around on a regular basis.

'Try to anticipate what your wife might want to know. You don't need to be a mind reader. But you can be accommodating, proactive and empathetic enough to help her avoid taking on a private investigator role. Remember, most wives don't want to be in that role and are incredibly disappointed in themselves when they adopt it.'[111]

Any man who is at all serious about repentance, restitution and his family's healing and wholeness would do well to read this book. We will discuss transparency and trust building in more detail in Chapter 16.

Martinkus isn't the only member of the New Life team with thought-provoking ideas about how to rebuild trust. Former sex addict turned counsellor, David Wever, compares rebuilding trust to rebuilding credit. 'It can be done, but only through a combination of time and consistency,' he explains.[112]

Martinkus likens trust building to creating a lego structure. Each trustworthy act by the addict adds another brick to a structure his wife can see. As the structure grows, so does her sense that it is safe to trust again.

Many men get frustrated at the amount of time it takes to rebuild trust, and how very easily they can destroy their new 'trust infrastructure'. If our husband is pushing for us to trust him, he's clearly not getting the concept. It might be time to share this, or Martinkus', book with him.

Also, it's important we don't let our husband confuse forgiveness with trust, and accuse us of sinning when we don't trust him. Forgiveness, which we will discuss in Chapter 15, is actually for the sake of the forgiver: for her freedom and relationship with God. At some point, every woman would do well to make a decision to begin the forgiveness process. However, some women will never, and should never, trust the addict again with such precious matters as her emotional safety, her children's safety, the family's finances, etc. If he has not become more trustworthy in these matters, she has every right, and would be well advised, to keep her distance and take matters into her own hands – prayerfully.

Lying is a sin. Not trusting a liar… is not.

Taking it Further

Do you believe your husband has disclosed everything about his addiction?

Do you want to know everything? Why or why not?

Do you feel supported by your husband and others with regards to the level of details you are asking for, or are you being told not to ask so many questions?

Is your husband being more honest in other areas of his life since coming out in the open about his addiction? If not, what might that indicate about his willingness to disclose everything you have asked him to?

Is your husband being patient with your trust journey? Is he willing to support it by being honest and transparent? Do you see increased spiritual commitment?

Do you believe God loves you? Do you believe He wants you and your children to be physically safe? What about emotionally safe?

For Reflection: Philippians 4:6-7 and Luke 12:2-3

Endnotes

103 M Magness, *Stop Sex Addiction: Real Hope, True Freedom for Sex Addicts and their Partners,* Central Recovery Press, 2013, p. 61.

104 2014/2105 Survey of Wives of Sex Addicts. 51% of respondents stated that their marriage was over.

105 J Condie, 'Should I Make My Husband Take a Polygraph Test?' Pure Intimacy, retrieved, September 2014 <http://www.pureintimacy. org/s/should-i-make-my-husband-take-a-polygraph-test/>.

106 B Steffens and R L Rennie, 'The Traumatic Nature of Disclosure for Wives of Sex Addicts', Taylor and Francis Group LLC, 2006.

107 M Means, 'To Snoop or Not to Snoop', retrieved September, 2014 <http://bit.ly/1I2HKt2>.

108 Holz, ibid.

109 Holz, ibid.

110 Means and Steffens, p. 219

111 Martinkus, *Worthy of Her Trust*, p. 93.

112 D Wever, 'Will she ever trust me again?' New Life Live, 2003, retrieved Oct. 2014 <http://newlife.com/will-she-ever-trust-me-again>.

'And you didn't get it from a toilet seat, no matter what anyone tells you.'

There's a bitter edge to my grandmother's voice. It catches me by surprise. Still, I'm relieved. She seems to get what I'm telling her... about why I walked away from my first marriage, and why I'm considering walking away from the second.

She passes me a tissue and takes one for herself. 'I know what it feels like to live with a cheating husband.'

'You... what?'

She hesitates a moment, lips tightening. 'Your grandfather,' she leans forward. 'I remember him coming home drunk one night and calling his mistress, begging her to let him come over. Then there was the time that one of the women's husbands burst through our door at dinner time and threatened your grandfather, saying he'd better stay away from his wife... right in front of the kids. Then there was all the...'

All these years I've been hiding the truth from my grandmother, assuming she was too naive and innocent to understand. My mother hid the fact of my father's infidelity from grandma ('mum' to her) as well. But, she knows. At the core of her being, she knows.

And it explains so much. Why such a godly, loving, giving woman hates her husband. For years I'd been seeing hints of it. But now – with him having just turned 90 and her in her mid-80's – she doesn't seem capable of holding it below the surface any more.

It came out recently as we talked about my grandfather's eternal destination. My grandmother explained that she had presented the 'gospel' to him recently and he had rebuffed her. By her tone I could tell she was quite okay with that result. It made me wonder what would happen if he did open himself to a relationship with Jesus. What would her reaction be if she arrived in heaven and found my grandfather waiting to greet her?

None too pleased, was my conclusion.

CHAPTER 10

Six Reactions to Infidelity

At the risk of over-generalising, I commonly see six types of reactions, in spouses, to betrayal and sexual addiction:

1. Staying and spiritualising
2. Staying and enabling
3. Staying and coping through our own addiction, revenge or medication
4. Leaving him and trying to forget about it
5. Leaving him and seeking healing for ourselves
6. Staying, with boundaries in place: seeking healing through God and others

Of course some women will explore the whole gamut of these reactions. Between my two marriages, I've hit most of them. Obviously only the last two can produce any healing and wholeness in our lives. However, the other four call out loudly to the broken-hearted and we should be very careful about judging women who fall into any of these traps.

Factors that affect our reaction include the family we were brought up in and how they coped with pain; our emotional maturity; our spiritual maturity; and our community's (e.g., church's) position on marriage, divorce and infidelity.

Let's take a closer look at the first four, unhealthy, reactions.

> Q: Why did you choose not to set boundaries?
> A: Fear of husband's response and the vows I took before God, family and friends.

Staying and Spiritualising

My grandmother was one of the kindest, most loving people you could hope to meet. That's a description that applies to many spiritualisers.[113] They give of themselves endlessly, serve others tirelessly.

However, my grandmother was dying inside. Festering wounds around my grandfather's infidelity and abuse were eating her alive. It was incredibly painful to see. And she was not alone.

Spiritualising is very easy to fall into when we lack the opportunity to process our pain. Moreover, it's a sin that crops up frequently in religious (as opposed to 'godly') cultures. It abounds in societies that are less tolerant of boundaries and consequences – and more condemning of divorce. These are all apt descriptions of the world my grandmother was raised in... the world many of today's older women grew up in.

But what exactly is 'spiritualising'?

No doubt there are a number of different definitions of this term. However, in my mind, spiritualising is the consistent practice of taking biblical precepts (and/or scripture) and twisting them to support unhealthy thinking and behaviour – even sin.

For example, many spiritualising wives use the principal of submission as a tool to justify ignoring their husband's addiction. Richard Blankenship states that (arguably) '…the most abused words in the bible are, "Wives submit to your husbands. As to the Lord".'[114] When it comes to the spiritual abuse of wives of addicts – and the wife excusing her own inaction – I suspect he's right.

For an excellent study on Ephesians 5 and 6 from a Hebrew point of view (because after all, Paul was a Hebrew) I recommend *God's Panoply*, by Anne Hamilton. In this book, Hamilton persuasively argues that the apostle Paul was trying to explain to his Greek readers the Hebrew concept of submission – an alien idea for which there was no equivalent in the Greek language. Says Hamilton, 'the concept was worse than alien: the nearest word in Greek had a meaning diametrically opposed to the corresponding Hebrew word.'

She points out that the problem arises when the Greek military term, *hupotasso*, "submit", in Paul's exhortation, 'Wives, submit to your husbands,' is taken out of its context. Isolating this phrase divorces it from Paul's extended explanation of the Hebrew concept *nasa'*, "uplift", from which arises the Hebrew words for "submission", "married", "armour-bearing", "forgiveness" and a host of related terms. In Hebrew, "submission" meant to lift another up.

Because a military connotation hangs over the word *hupotasso*, Hamilton suggests Paul was also tying it into the concept of the Jewish covenant defender, or armour-bearer. Thus a better translation of 'Wives, submit to your husbands,' in her view is: 'Wives, lift up your husbands – be their companions for battle.'

She adds,

'The importance of uplift in relation to covenant submission is repeatedly demonstrated even today in the symbolism of both the Jewish wedding and the bar mitzvah. Because the Hebrew word for "married" derives from nasa', *"lift up", the newlyweds are lifted up on chairs in the hora dance. Because the bar mitzvah is the time when a boy becomes a "son of the covenant", he is lifted up on the shoulders of his father... Paul's careful explanation of what real submission means is peppered with ideas relating to* nasa'. *To ignore the Hebrew background is to put both women and family down, when it was his clear intention to lift them up, just as Christ had done.'*[115]

Hamilton's ideas fit very nicely with Dr Cloud's and Dr Townsend's views of submission as described in *Boundaries in Marriage*. Here the doctors explain that submission is always to be done in love – love in its fullest meaning. Thus submission is not doing everything our husbands tell us to; rather, it means upholding our responsibility to love our spouse no matter what. That means loving them enough to say, 'That's wrong!' sometimes, or to create a boundary of space by removing ourselves if there is abuse or betrayal.[116]

'Wives lift up (support, forgive, carry, fight alongside) your husbands as to the Lord' and do it in authentic love, rings truer to me. It seems to better incorporate God's grace-filled nature and His just love. However, in many ways the Hebrew understanding of submission is more challenging than the Greek concept 'do what you're told'. God's definition of love is more challenging than our modern notion of 'give him whatever he wants'.

Each woman will have to work out with the Holy Spirit how this plays out in life with a sex addict. However, it doesn't seem to leave a lot of place for ignoring or enabling sinful behaviour and excusing it with whatever bible verse seems to back us up.

> I first realised I had options when a counsellor told me 3.5 years ago, 'You have been a faithful wife for 35 years, you don't have to do it anymore.' I responded, 'Yes I do, I am a Christian.' Her response [to that] set me free for the first time in my life. — survey respondent

Spiritualising as 'The Martyr' and 'The Rescuer'

Some women (I may have been one of them) choose to stay with an addict and adopt a self-righteous attitude. I suspect that the 'superior martyr' position is a tactic for shielding our hearts: particularly when the addict in question is unenthusiastic about (or even set against) changing.

Says Townsend: 'Victimhood is characterised by three tendencies: a sense of globalised helplessness to act and make things better, a focus on the "bad other", and the perception of moral superiority.'[117] None of these tendencies leads us, or 'the baddie' toward health and wholeness.

Some of the 2014/2015 Survey respondents stated that they'd hoped their husband would change out of gratitude for their self-sacrifices and obvious suffering. This is rarely the case. We cannot 'give' enough to make him love us. He must grow, heal and choose to love us.

'Okay,' we may be tempted to argue, 'our husbands may not love us more… but God will love us more then for our sacrificial giving? Right?'

God says He loves us because we are his children made in his image, not for what we do. And He wants us to love Him the same way. He could certainly command our love (force it) but he wants us to love Him out of our free will.

Says Townsend, after quoting Deutoronomy 4:29,

'God has no interest in fear-based obedience; he knows it has no meaning. God wants to be loved, and he made you in his image so that you also want to be loved. But love never develops without freedom, and so there is always risk.'[118]

Trying to work our way into someone's heart is ultimately just a form of manipulation. The sad reality is that many of our husbands are not capable of loving anyone – not even themselves.

The good news is that we have a God who loves us unconditionally. He made us free to love Him and others in return.

> Q: Top regrets?
> A: ... [I] had public sex... dressed up for him... permitted him to take photos of me during sex as well as posing nude... – survey respondent

Staying and Enabling

With those definitions of submission in mind, what do we do when our husbands tell us they want us to be sexier in the bedroom? Is it lifting him up (spiritually, ladies – spiritually) to comply? Is it loving him, supporting him and fighting alongside him when we encourage him in a practice that may cause him to slide further down the road to eternal destruction?

When it came to listing their regrets 11% of the 2014/2015 Survey respondents admitted that they had allowed themselves to be persuaded to participate in their husband's addiction. I believe this figure to be on the low side. Many of the women I have walked with on this journey have fallen into complicity with their addict/husband in this area: usually after being told by their husband that if things were just a little hotter, he wouldn't struggle so much.

Martinkus devotes a whole chapter in *Worthy of Her Trust* to the myth that either more sex or 'the porn star experience' kind of sex will help a man remain faithful, or recover faster from his addiction.

'Increasing frequency of sexual intercourse with one's wife usually serves only to create an expanded context for acting out. Now, in addition to a computer, a hotel room, an office, or a strip club being the place where sexual misconduct occurs, it also takes place in the marriage bed. The husband's view of his wife changes from seeing her as a beautiful child of God and dearly treasured companion, to viewing her as another object... Moreover when a wife agrees to do sex differently, meaning more "exciting" or "exotic" by

trying different positions, clothing, conversation, or implements, she simply becomes an equivalent of the husband's debilitating porn, a personal prostitute… Asking his wife to heighten the sexual arousal experience serves only to strengthen the unhealthy neural pathways that perpetuate the addiction… The neural networks associated with those thought patterns affect intimacy on every level, maintain self-preservation, activate consequences-avoidance techniques (perpetuating further lies) and are connected to the kind of compartmentalisation that allows someone to live a duplicitous life.[119]

In other words, to submit to his request to 'spice it up' is to help keep him in his sin. There is no way to justify this type of decision. If any man or woman says perverse sexual behaviour is covered under 'submission', they need to back up a bit earlier in Chapter 5 of Ephesians where it says:

But among you there must not be even a hint of sexual immorality, or of any kind of impurity, or of greed, because these are improper for God's holy people… For of this you can be sure: No immoral, impure or greedy person–such a person is an idolater–has any inheritance in the kingdom of Christ and of God. Let no one deceive you with empty words, for because of such things God's wrath comes on those who are disobedient. Therefore do not be partners with them. –Ephesians 5:3-4,6

When women are seduced into playing the seductress, it's usually due to a belief that sex will heal the relationship. There is a degree of truth to this idea. Sex has been designed by God to be healing, fulfilling, and bonding (more in Chapter 17). However, it's only sex *His* way that will accomplish this. As pastor and international speaker Gordon Dalbey says in *Pure Sex: The Spirituality of Desire*, 'Ultimately, sex apart from surrender to the God who created it distracts from His purpose and at worst, sabotages it.'[120]

If you have fallen into this trap, like so many of your sisters, God's forgiveness awaits. Don't let shame hold you back. Do, however, repent and refuse to continue in this path. You are harming yourself, your husband and your relationship if you don't stop.

Martinkus relates how both husband and wife can find true healing via their sexuality:

'Ultimately what we're shooting for is not just stopping his acting out and having more sex within the marriage. The goal is to experience sexuality in a way that honours God and each other. We're aiming for an experience of knowing and being known so intimately that it bonds our souls together.'[121]

See more on sexual intimacy in Chapter 17.

Coping Through Addiction

Alcohol, food, (illegal) drugs, and shopping topped the list of addictions that wives of addicts admitted – in the 2014/2015 Survey – falling prey to.[122] For some women, there was an isolated incident of using the substance (particularly alcohol) following a traumatic incident around their husband's betrayal. For others, addiction – particularly with food – is a daily battle.

Other addictions that didn't come up as often, but which I am aware are all too common, are 'my own sexual addiction,' media (especially TV and romance novels) and affairs.

As regards the latter, sometimes this plays out as a one-time revenge affair. At other times, it's simply a woman, with battered self-esteem, falling prey to more wolves in sheeps' clothing. Fortunately, it seems that far more women consider having a physical (as opposed to internet) affair than actually do – 5% (considered) vs 3% (actual) according to the 2014/2015 Survey. I suspect that almost every woman who has had an affair, as a result of her pain, has regretted it very quickly. That was certainly my experience following the break-up of my first marriage.

As regards legal medication, please keep in mind that when we approach it with the 'make the pain stop, because I don't want to have to change anything in my life' attitude, we may also be setting ourselves up for problems, including a potential addiction.

One of the issues with addictions and medication is that they can soothe us and give us a false sense of peace and safety, when we are not necessarily safe. When our children are not necessarily safe. I have seen this backfire on women many times. Thus, it's not unusual to hear the addict, when his wife comes off of medication or gets help for her addiction, complain that she needs to: go back on her meds/go shopping, eat a chocolate bar, etc. As one survey respondent said,

'[Brand-name anti-depressant] helped me focus more and stay in the present. In fact I went back to school and… worked out at the gym 3 to 4 times a week. Unfortunately my husband used this time while I was out of the house to start bringing them [prostitutes] to our bedroom.'

In at least one case I witnessed a woman's inability to monitor the situation (for the safety of her daughter) resolved when she asked the physician to reduce the dosage of her current medication. Those on medication should not be afraid to seek feedback from safe people about whether they are 'under reacting' to new information or 'throwing caution to the wind.'

Coping with Him

The reason addictive behaviours are listed as 'regrets' is clearly because women are aware that these are unhealthy decisions. They realise that it would be better to cope with God's power in their life: they just don't know how to make Him their refuge when they are hurting so badly.

I wish there was a formula I could insert here that would tell you how to do it. There isn't. I don't even know for sure how I fumbled my way to God and didn't fall into addiction, revenge, etc. as part of my second betrayal journey. There were times when numbing the pain sure sounded good. There were times when the comfort of food seemed tempting.

All I can say is keep crying out to Him. He is listening. Soak in words of scripture about his compassion and reflect on the fact that He does care.

Also, try and find sisters to talk to who can relate that love and care to you. Seek out spiritual mentors who understand that Jesus made it a priority 'to bind up the brokenhearted, to proclaim freedom for the captives and release from darkness for the prisoners.' –Isaiah 61:1.

> 'My life has improved significantly. I have peace with myself, with family and friends. I do my work better and my finances have improved.'
> — survey respondent, who has left her addict husband

Leaving and Trying to Forget

Ah glorious peace. 51% of the respondents to the 2014/2015 Survey are no longer with their husbands. 84% of them say they initiated a separation/divorce (either temporary or permanent). The number one benefit of no longer being with their addicted spouse cited by respondents: peace.

I experienced this after my first marriage. When the triggers disappear, we know the children are safe, and we don't have to think about 'what is he doing tonight to break my heart', life seems so much safer.

However, just as sobriety doesn't equal recovery, so getting out of the line of fire doesn't heal the bullet wounds. It's frequently a fine first step, but there is still a healing work that needs to be done.

Moreover, separation can propel an addict to action. When that's the case, healing of the relationship becomes a distinct possibility. Simply leaving and cutting off contact until the end of time may seem easier; but is it what's best for all parties? Is it what God has for us?

Leaving Space for the Marriage

Counsellor Milan Yerkovich tells wives of abusive (including addicted) husbands that a separation can be a means by which we tell the 'non-compliant partner... that their behaviour is unacceptable.'[123] He calls this a restorative type of separation: one where we hope to evoke change and then reconcile.

Thus we don't need to see 'moving out' as the end of the relationship. Of course, in many cases it will be. If our husband is not prepared to change his unacceptable behaviours – including his unfaithfulness or abuse – the separation should become permanent.

It's a tough balance to strike: not holding on to what Dr Townsend calls 'vain hope' – which can thwart our healing – and yet remaining open to miracles.

Townsend puts it this way:

'I have seen many dead connections resurrected. So be open to the possibility. But let go. You can enter sadness and still leave a door open at the same time. It sounds like it can't be done, but it can in this way: you are putting your energy and focus into the next steps and the next relationships. But... if God miraculously changes the situation, you can respond to that. Move ahead, but let God be God.'[124]

When a woman has long tolerated her husband's addiction (too long for her own health), she is more likely to want the separation to be 'the end'. That's a very natural sentiment for a thoroughly grieved and frustrated woman to take. However, I would counsel a woman to be open (at least for the next 12 months) to the possibility of God using the situation to bring her husband to a crisis that causes true repentance and the initiation of a recovery journey. That said, the onus should be on him (and if he's sincere God will help him in this) to prove that things are changing and to begin re-building trust.

I frequently find myself wishing women would take a stronger stand earlier on in their journey: when there are fewer wounds and the addict is less mired down in his addiction. Then the separation would have a better chance of promoting healing for both parties: individually and as a couple. However, no matter what the past has been like, God is still God and nothing is impossible for him.

Our healing is, in itself, a miracle. Our marriage? It's in God's hands.

Working Our Recovery

Dr Sheri Keffer, who runs *Women in the Battle* seminars as part of the Every Man's Battle ministry did an excellent interview that helps illuminate what healing should look like for spouses of addicts who find themselves single. The interview was with Karene, the ex-wife of a sex addict with very abusive tendencies. Karene talks about her post-divorce healing journey as involving:

- **Counselling** - with a specialist counsellor and with a commitment to be brave and authentic in the sessions. Karene's sessions included EMDR (Eye movement desensitization and reprocessing) therapy for PTSD.
- **Support Group** - regular attendance in a specialist group for betrayed wives, or wives of sex addicts, and friendships with other betrayed wives. In the words of Richard Blankenship: 'Healing doesn't take place in isolation.'
- **God** - Says Karene: 'God really rescued me, and that's because I ran to Him with open arms and He accepted me… He is there and He really means [it when] He says He wants that personal relationship.'[125]

Trying to forget how wounded we are is just setting us up for more relational issues in the future. Let's not let surface-level peace fool us. We can take time to grieve our losses and process them with God and others.

God wants to redeem what has happened to us, using it to make us wiser, stronger, more mature and more truly at peace – in all circumstances.

Taking it Further

Has your husband ever coerced or tried to coerce you into supporting his addiction? If you went along, how did this make you feel? If you didn't, how did it make you feel? Have you ever discussed this situation with a safe person?

If you have not discussed it, consider that many wives of addicts have done something related to their spouse's addiction they are ashamed of. One of the first steps to dispelling shame is bringing our sins (or actions) into the light. Consider asking God to bring a safe person into your life with whom to share this part of your story.

Are you aware that God forgives you and wants to free you from the pain of the shame? Ask Him to bring that understanding deep into your heart. Then take a moment to repent and as you do, ask Him to destroy both the sin and the shame.

Do you feel you must stay in your marriage (no matter where your husband is and what he does) because of your faith?

Write a letter to God about how the idea of leaving makes you feel. Ask Him how it makes Him feel.

Do you feel you must flee your marriage though there is no immediate threat to you or your children and your husband appears (most of the time) to be genuinely remorseful and engaged in the recovery process?

Write a letter to God about how the idea of staying makes you feel. Ask Him how it makes Him feel.

Are you tempted to turn to another man for validation? Have you tried talking to God about that feeling and asking Him to show you how He feels about you?

> ## For Reflection: Song of Solomon 6:3

Endnotes

113 That said, some spiritualisers are controlling and abusive, excusing their bad behaviour by using scripture or by citing 'higher spiritual' reasons.

114 Blankenship, pp. 84–85.

115 A Hamilton, personal interview, 20 December, 2014.

116 Cloud and Townsend, ibid. pp. 484–487.

117 Townsend, ibid, p. 75.

118 Townsend, ibid, p. 228.

119 Martinkus, ibid, p. 48-50.

120 G Dalbey, '*Pure Sex: The Spirituality of Desire*', Civitas Press, San Jose, 2014, ebook, p. 156.

121 Martinkus, ibid, p. 51.

122 8% of survey respondents listed some form of substance abuse or addiction as their dearest regret.

123 M Yerkovich, 'Ask Me Anything', New Life TV, Oct 10, 2014.

124 Townsend adds that women can begin this process — of grieving and moving on — while still living with the addict. [Townsend, ibid, pp. 152–153].

125 S Keffer, 'A Battle Veteran's Testimony', New Life TV, Nov 11, 2014.

I groan. The pain has drawn me out of my drugged sleep again. I am lying on my back looking up into the dark. Each breath is unbearable. I have to go empty my bladder, but I can't imagine how I can move. There is a searing pain in my right shoulder blade. Like a knife so deep I can feel it in my lungs.

I try to shift my position. Burning, tearing pain. Tears of agony stream down my face. I'd wanted to die... but this way?

The events leading to this moment started a couple of months ago when I'd overheard M tell his counsellor (they weren't taking great pains not to be heard) that large breasts were what he particularly sought out in porn.

Of all the traumas I have faced in my life, that moment was one of the worst.

That will not be comprehensible to most women, but then most women have breasts... I don't. My lack of breasts has been the source of my most painful rejections. Those rejections came from various sources: my mother, who made embarrassed remarks to sales clerks; a male friend, who asked if had I considered getting surgery; numerous women in gym or theatrical changing rooms, who with their derisive looks, stares and giggles used my deficiency to make themselves feel superior; and my sister-in-law, who commented one night after dinner how shocking it was that I could breastfeed considering I have the smallest breasts she has ever seen. She's a La Leche League (think, 'Nursing Mothers of Australia') leader.

I could go on. My lack of breasts has been a source of indescribable pain to me. My first husband started chasing around after our Double D cup babysitter (including snapping photos of her) the last year of our marriage. Now, I'd learned that I was the exact opposite of M's 'type' (his word).

Two weeks ago I started to try and deal with the festering wound, so I pressed him for more information on the breast thing. He snapped and said, 'breasts are the only thing that do it for me. Yours are a turn off.'

I made it to the bathroom before collapsing. The next thing I remember, I was cleaning the toilet... with his toothbrush. (Yup, really.)

I was bedroom-bound for the next few days. I sat on the floor weeping and fantasising about running a knife through my chest. I went and fetched a knife from the kitchen several times. One night I slept with it. Thoughts of my little girl growing up without a mother, though, always seemed to rise above the pain.

So, after three days, I put the knife back in the block and got on the internet. I'd come up with another way to run a knife through my chest. Another way to bring my emotional pain into the realm of the physical.

I've been home from surgery three days and I can still barely move. The pain in my chest is unlike anything I've ever known. Because of my 'lack' the surgeon put the small implants under the muscles of my chest wall. He warned me that I'd need a serious barrage of painkillers to get through this.

The pills help with the pains deep in my chest and the ones on my skin – where, the long knife wounds under each of my, now, B-cup breasts glare angry, red and jagged. Infinitely worse than these pains, though, is the pain in my right shoulder blade. It robs me of sleep, mobility, and at times, the ability to draw breath.

I am on my knees shuffling toward the toilet, my knees wet from the trail of tears I'm leaving. Numerous times since he has come out, I've visualised M thrusting a knife into my back. Now, I'm living it.

CHAPTER 11

Valley of the Shadow

Sometimes women judge each other's pain. This comes up at times in support groups: 'Well, at least your husband only looked at porn. Mine was sleeping with prostitutes.'

As spouses' coach, Shelley Martinkus, says: 'Her pain is her pain…We cannot judge each other's pain.' She and husband Jason, in their video, *Why Does it Hurt So Much?* point out that when it comes to pain, the story of our life (including its traumas, false beliefs, previous betrayals) contributes to the pain of the moment.[126]

I had experienced numerous instances of being put down by people because of my small chest size. However, I was bearing up pretty well under it all. Though many people (again family, 'friends'… men I barely knew) had asked me why I didn't just get an operation, I was pretty good at dismissing them. Until the day my husband threw in his lot with them.

Why that undid me, to the point that I would turn to a form of self-mutilation, I can't even begin to explain. The discovery that he held me, and my body, in contempt just tipped me over an edge I'd been teetering on for weeks.

> I took a suitcase and my dog and left because I felt suicidal. I knew if I stayed, one way or another I was going to physically die. Emotionally I could only feel pain and grief to have the person I once considered to be my protector, my safe place, and best friend treat me the way he did. It felt like I had been stabbed in the heart over and over and was bleeding to death.
>
> — survey respondent

Intimacy Murdered

It is psychologically crushing to make oneself vulnerable – naked and welcoming – only to be resoundingly rejected.

Whether or not our husband has told us directly in words, 'you're insufficient, your gift isn't good enough,' he has told us indirectly with his infidelity. Therein lies, I feel, our core emotional and psychological wound.

Numerous times in my early adult years I was told about the 'delicate male psyche' in the area of sexuality. Books I read said a woman must always affirm her husband in his sexuality: to fail to do so was the ultimate cruelty and would result in severe damage to the man and the marriage.

No one ever talked about how cruel such a blow would be for the woman. Perhaps because most of these books were written by men who lacked the female perspective on the subject. Perhaps because women are expected to show more resilience than men.

There is no 'bounce back' from this blow, however. Women, when describing the pain, almost to a one use images of extreme violence. With God's help, nevertheless, we can survive, and in time get beyond the devastation.

Some women, of course, do not experience an intense emotional reaction. They must still be watchful, however, as their reaction may simply be delayed or it may manifest as other symptoms: anger, violence, depression, desperation to get into another relationship, etc.

Self-Image and Self-Esteem

In May 2015 I conducted a survey, in conjuction with A Circle of Joy, specifically on the effects of discovery of a husband's sexual addiction on the wife's body image. 96% of the 73 respondents reported that their body image had been negatively impacted by discovery of the betrayal. When asked to rate their pain, around their damaged body image, on a scale of 0 to 100, 70% rated it above 50. Many of these women were already years into their healing journey.[127]

Dr Sheri Keffler, in her interview with ex-wife of an addict, Karene (see Chapter 9), says that women need to work with others to deconstruct their false beliefs that have sprung up as a result of what's happened to them. This includes such beliefs as 'I'm not valuable, I'm unimportant, I'm ugly, my body is hateful...'[128]

What my husband said to me about breasts made me feel uniquely ugly and objectionable. Like I was sub-human: cursed in a way no other woman is. I began to feel so ashamed of my body that I wanted to die. I felt others wanted me to die.

The enemy loves to isolate us.

What reshaped my thinking was a conversation with one of my near-adult sons about how we'd feel if people told his, then nine-year-old, sister she was ugly. To us she is uniquely beautiful and precious. But what if she believed these (hypothetical) other people rather than us? The idea seemed too horrendous to consider.

Do we think God's reaction is any different when others tell us we are ugly and despicable? Even if it's many others (like our whole warped society) who are telling us this?

His voice may be the only one speaking truth on the matter. The challenge: can we hone in on His words? Can we give them more weight than the voice of the enemy around us? Is it possible God wants to help us in that challenge by having us flee the lies (and liars) and seek out those who speak His truth?

God's truth: you are unique, special, beautiful and loved. Satan's load of crap: you are uniquely contemptible, ugly, despised.

....

Q: What helped you overcome your depression/ suicidal ideation?

A: The love I have for my children, parents, my sister, and niece; and my awareness of their love for me. And the faith that God will never let me go. He will be faithful to the end. — survey respondent

....

Depression and Suicide

93% of respondents to the 2014/2015 Survey of Wives of Sex Addicts said they felt depressed as a result of their husband's betrayal. Moreover, more than a third of respondents (36%) said they felt suicidal at times.

Doctors will tell us that ongoing depression is a biochemical issue. As much as that may be true, the bible looks at it from the point of view of the heart: 'Hope deferred makes the heart sick.' –Proverbs 13:12

When a crisis as profound as marital betrayal sweeps into our lives (or death, sudden loss, etc.), destroying many of our hopes and dreams, it's not unusual for depression to result. From there, a person may become 'passively suicidal'. Actively suicidal is the next step: the one where action is taken toward ending one's life.

According to the World Health Organisation, 1 million people/year take their life.[129] Approximately 3000 of those deaths occur in Australia and New Zealand.[130] Thus, suicide is not as uncommon as people think. So what do we do when we or someone we love is suicidal?

If someone is actively suicidal – that is, they're going to do something immediately – we need to call for intervention (i.e. the police, hospital, mental health professional, suicide prevention line). If we are in that state ourselves, we should reach out to a professional or someone who we know loves us and has offered solid support and counsel in the past.

Of course reaching out when we are actively suicidal is easier said than done. As Dr Keffer says, 'It is a natural reaction to hide away and not… talk to anybody because of feeling so overwhelmed by all the shame, numbness, shock. One of the hardest things to do is not to isolate.'[131]

The same is true for those who are passively suicidal or depressed. However, reaching out to those who can listen and offer comfort and hope is the wisest choice.

If it is not us who is in this state, but rather someone we are walking with, listening is the best thing we can do. 'They [the hurting],' says Keffer, 'need to be allowed to tell their story… in whatever way they want to.'[132]

Dr Townsend adds a challenge here. 'In our Christian faith, we're not good listeners. We want to have the good story, the victory story, the positive story… but there's a time it says in the bible, to comfort those who need comfort.'

In *God's Power to Change*, John and Paula Sandford give Christians a list of 'don'ts' when it comes to ministering to those who are depressed (including suicidal). They include:

- Don't say, 'cheer up'
- Don't take the person to a party, worship service, prayer meeting or out for light-hearted entertainment
- Don't give advice
- Don't try to exorcise/engage in spiritual warfare with the person regarding a spiritual side to the depression
- Don't tell them to pray/read the bible more

Those of us acquainted with depression will know how true this advice is.

So what do we do to help others? What do we look for from others?

Availability and compassion. We 'weep with those who weep.'

Beyond this, Dr Townsend says there are three things that can positively impact someone who is passively suicidal. That is demonstrating:

- Somebody gets it… the one hurting is not alone with her feelings
- She has choices … they may not be great ones, but they are choices
- The future is not necessarily permanently as it is today (i.e., there is hope)[133]

Townsend, Keffer, Blankenship, Means and other top therapists also recommend EMDR therapy for those struggling with ongoing depression and suicidal ideation in the wake of a traumatic event.

> I still get depressed at times, but I have used the anger/depression to move me to action in preparation to leave my husband (who doesn't think he has a problem and blames me). I have hope for my future, but no hope for my marriage. — survey respondent

Don't Do the Undoable

In the early days of my trauma crisis my mother sat me down and said, 'I always tell the wives of my clients in recovery not to make any un-doable decisions for the next 12 months, unless it is for the sake of safety. As they get healing and their partner gets healing, they won't be the same person six months from now that they are today. They certainly won't be the same person in 12 months.'

As regards the operation: I really wish I had listened to her. While it was not exactly 'un-doable' my body and my heart will always be scarred from the experience. That's not to say that such an operation is wrong in all cases: but it was wrong for me. While it has offered me some small degree of comfort in that I'm not gawked at any more by women (or men), it has been a stumbling block in my marriage (as I won't let M 'benefit' from the change). Moreover, I know that some day I'll have to tell my daughter how I couldn't stand up for the body God gave me – one similar to her now developing body.

Likewise, making an undoable decision about the marriage or harming ourselves can have devastating ramifications for us and our loved ones. A death in the family: terrible and painful. A suicide in the family: worse. Rather than having a community of people come around us to offer support in our grief, the family of someone who has committed suicide is often shunned by others.

We need to hold on to the hope that we will not be the same person in 12 months: particularly if we are pursuing healing. Let's hold on to the love God has for us. Let's reach out.

If it has been more than 12 months and we feel that our depression still pushes us toward being actively suicidal on a regular basis, it's imperative we reach out to safe people (if we have not already done so). If we are able to, we can begin looking at our choices with others who can help us evaluate our situation. Our pain may seem insurmountable and our situation hopeless, but as long as there is a God in heaven, it isn't. That is just our current perspective, based on lies from the enemy of our soul, and the traumatic experience we have undergone.

This pain can be overcome with the help of God and community. Dr Townsend says there's a difference between a wound and a scar. The goal, when betrayal has left us depressed and/or suicidal, is to work with God and others so our actively bleeding wounds are transformed into scars.[134]

> Q: Top regrets?
> A: Sharing with people who turned out to be very unsafe
> — survey respondent

When Reaching Out is Unsafe

There will be instances when those we reach out to are unsafe and add to our pain. I suffered this extreme crisis with my husband in my first four weeks in my new country. I had virtually no connections here and my connections back home seemed to be dissolving quickly.

Nevertheless I tried on multiple occasions to reach out to women. This included:

- A Christian neighbour whose husband was also addicted to porn. She had strong co-dependent traits (her mother has been in multiple marriages to physically abusive men, her husband was from a family of abusive men). She spiritualised to the point where she saw it as against biblical submission to keep the password to the computer hidden from her husband (though *he* was asking us for help to block his access to online porn).
- The wife of an addict who, though a lovely person, had not processed her pain. In our first meeting she made a comment about her unattractive, flat-chested daughter.
- Wives of the men in my husband's group – they refused to meet me.
- A counsellor who, during our first meeting, told me my husband was abusive (true), would never be attracted to me (not true) and I should leave him (not for her to decide).

All this time I was trying to find a church where I might get help and support. Since many of the women down under dress in a more sexualised manner than we were accustomed to, I felt continually triggered.

After a couple months, my husband gave up on church as he felt it was hurting his recovery. Even my sons said they were struggling with their purity – because of all the cleavage, legs, curves and midriffs – and would no longer attend. For quite some time, we were a 'home-church only' family.

Since making safe, healthy connections wasn't going well for me, I reached out to family: my mum and grandmother. The distance, however, made that impractical at times.

What was I learning? 'Reaching out is futile.'

To make things worse, M kept telling his friends about my trauma reactions and reporting back to me their responses: statements like, 'I wouldn't put up with that.'

Despite this underwhelming show of support for my pain and vulnerability, I continued to try to connect, emailing one of my friends from my old hometown. A single woman, but wise in the things of the Lord and full of grace, she was wonderful. However, at my lowest points, obstacles like the time difference, the impersonal nature of email and a lack of affordable telecommunications technology (on both our ends) seemed too great to overcome.

> I have always been a spiritual person and for me it just felt natural drawing closer to God during my healing process. God is my source of strength, stability.
>
> — survey respondent

Just God

Of course there were, as I would discover within the next year, online resources I could have reached out to. There were also help lines I could have contacted. But, at this time of despair and ignorance, I couldn't muster enough will to do the research.

Thus, I perceived I was alone with God in this. It truly did not feel like enough in the days following my husband's abusive remarks, and I told Him so.

One day, at my very lowest I said to God that I needed him to send me some tangible sign of his love right then and there. Otherwise, I wouldn't be able to go on (I was actively suicidal).

I was sitting on the floor of my bedroom, hands to my face, weeping. The next instant, I felt a tear slip through my fingers and splash heavily on my trousers. In my spirit I felt something shift. I parted my hands and looked down. On my light-coloured pants, just above my knee, was that single splash. It had formed a perfectly symmetrical heart.

Sorrow meets love.

We need people. On days we feel our hopes are in the grave – our hearts too – we need to reach out. But sometimes there's just God. The God who tells us He is collecting our tears in a bottle.

He has been to the grave and back. If He is all we have, we can know He is enough.

Emergency Information

If you or someone you know is suicidal (passive or active) please keep the following numbers on hand:

Lifeline: 13 11 14 - https://www.lifeline.org.au

Lifeline Aotearoa: 09 909 8750 - http://www.lifeline.org.nz

Please see the resources section at the back of this book as well for more information on places you can find safe people to reach out to.

Taking it Further

There are those, including some therapists, who are not comfortable with the idea of anyone 'walking through the valley of the shadow of death.' Some will try to push anyone with suicidal ideations toward the psych ward, when this may not yet be called for. In a litigious world, no one wants to be held legally (or morally) responsible for someone else being hurt.

From the survey, and from other sources (including my own experience), I am aware that many wives of addicts live fairly constantly with a strong desire for the Lord to come back soon, take them away, etc. Sometimes this dull sensation becomes pointed – acute. The length of time the acute sensation of 'get me out of here' lasts tends to decrease the further we move away from our point of initial trauma. That said, it's common for it to flare up again when we are triggered.

Is it possible that living with a longing for the next world (i.e., suicidal ideation or being passively suicidal), is not quite so very pathological? Is it possible that we, with God's help and the help of our usual support network, can muddle our way through these periods (assuming they correct themselves after a few days)?

Did Jesus ever feel this way? (Answer: see Mathew 17:17)

> *For Reflection*: Psalm 56
> (especially verse 8) and Psalm 23

Endnotes

126 Martinkus and Martinkus, 'Why Does it Hurt So Much', ibid.

127 For more on the results of the body image survey, see the Beyond Betrayal Blog: www.beyondbetrayal.community.

128 S Keffler, 'A Battle Veteran's Testimony', New Life TV, Nov 11, 2014.

129 Retrieved September 2014. <www.befrienders.org/suicide-statistics>.

130 Australian statistics, based on data from 2012, from Mindframe-media. info. New Zealand statistics, based on data from 2012/2013: 'Six Fewer Suicides, But Figures Still Shock', *New Zealand Herald*, Sept 3, 2013.

131 Keffer and Townsend, 'Survivors After Suicide', New Life TV, August 25, 2014.

132 ….

133 ….

134 ….

I look at M's face and my heart sinks into my stomach. Guilt and shame are etched there.

'What?' my jaw aches with tension as I prepare for the blow.

'There was this really attractive girl at the hardware store checkout. I didn't notice her until it was my turn to pay. I had my glasses off so I assumed it was an older woman like usual.'

'What did you do?'

'I bit my tongue, like they taught us in group. I started praying for her too. Then I ran to the car and concentrated on focusing my sexuality on you – you know, like they taught us.'

'Mmm. Did you lust after her?'

'No, definitely... well, maybe. I'm not sure. Not like I used to. I wasn't trying to.'

'Well, I guess that's... something.'

M looks down at his hands. 'Sorry. I wish it was better. You know though,' he meets my gaze again, 'when I was in the car, I started thinking about your legs... and I realised that I'm attracted to you too!'

My heart sinks lower. Wow, 'me too'. I don't say it out loud because I don't want to squelch his enthusiasm over this discovery. But somehow, it just doesn't seem like what I signed up for.

Is this as good as it gets?

CHAPTER 12

Good Enough

The line 'forsaking all others,' is part of the marriage vows for a reason. Who among us wouldn't walk away from the altar if our betrothed wanted that line omitted; or worse, wanted it altered to, 'forsaking *some* others'?

In today's society fewer and fewer men are able to live up to the vows they took at the altar. They have been trained (by the media, sometimes their own fathers), to look for a partner they find 'hot'. When that chemistry naturally fades, they look for it elsewhere: because that's what relationships with women are about… right? (More on this in Chapter 18.)

Many of us long for that Song of Solomon lover/husband. That's why when our husband says, 'I gave up the porn, prostitutes, affair partner, etc. isn't that enough?' it just doesn't sit well. Even in cases like mine, where the husband is trying, but unable to, completely walk away from the lusting, it still feels tremendously wounding.

Accepting that the passionate intimacy Solomon describes awaits us only in heaven is hard. For numerous women the death of their dreams, of being passionately loved, is the near-unbearable reality their depression centres on.

What is Lusting?

As part of processing my pain around my husband's problem with lusting, I've tried for years to understand what exactly lusting is. My husband tried multiple times to explain it to me. At first, he was less than honest about it, in an attempt to manipulate me into behaviour he was more comfortable with.

But as he felt safer with me, he gave me more details. He also shared the ideas on the subject found in books such as Fred Stoeker's and Steve Arterburn's *Every Man's Battle*.

It got me closer, but I still didn't get it… and I really wanted to. Like many women I've falsely believed at times, 'if I can just understand this thing, then it won't hurt.'

Finally, two weeks before I was due to write this chapter, I said to God, 'If you want me to describe lusting to women, you're going to have to help me find the information. Everything I've seen so far just doesn't quite compute for me.'

Within a few days of that prayer, I had a dream.

In the dream I was putting on my togs (i.e., 'swimmers' or 'swimming costume') and suddenly noticed that they were far more revealing than I normally tolerate. Then I realised I was already out in the pool area, and there were many men around me. I tried to cover up with my arms, but the sides of my breasts were still showing.

Then it was as if I was in the heads of a few of the men around me… this happened one at a time. The first one looked at me, saw the skin-covered bulge and immediately I experienced a small burst of sexual arousal. The man looked away instantly and clamped on that feeling in his brain. This happened with the other men. They experienced varying levels of sexual arousal hit before bouncing their eyes and clamping down on the arousal sensation. I could feel the annoyance of the last man. He was *not* looking for this. None of them were. This was their brain's natural reaction to the skin/curve combination and at least this last guy was fighting it tooth and nail.

Then the dream shifted and I was watching a high school girl's choir with M. I could see he was focused on one teen in particular. She was modestly dressed in a floral-print dress. My point of view shifted and I was in M's mind. I could see him seeking out the curves – though they weren't readily obvious. I looked through his eyes as he studied the girl's figure. Suddenly, she moved in a way that for a moment accentuated the shape of one buttock. He pounced on that and got his hit. I had the distinct sense that this young woman had just been robbed.

When I described the dream to my husband, he said that sounded correct. This was the way lusting worked as far as he's experienced it. There is both active and passive lusting. The active is akin to robbing and violating a woman. In fact, M went on to explain, 'It's kind of like a man walking up to you, looking around for the best angle, and taking a photo. Now that man can walk away with an imprint of your body parts on his brain and use it later to keep getting sexual arousal hits off of, or even to masturbate to.'

And as much as the passive lusting sounds completely innocent in my description, I didn't get the sense that the men in the dream were entirely off the hook. As the inappropriately dressed person in the scenario, yes, I was more culpable than they. However, I can't shake the sense that they did in fact play some role as well. Perhaps their porn re-wired brains were 'noticing' me, as Jason Martinkus puts it in his excellent article: 'Looking, Noticing, and Seeing'.[135]

Did these men sin?

That's not for me to decide.

Whether they did or not, I felt sorry for them. In any case, I'm with Dr Struthers who likes to take these 'Is it sin?' conversations into a new realm. He says we'd be better off asking, 'Did it bring you toward or away from sanctification?'.[136]

Questions like 'is it sin to lust, if you didn't do it actively (but didn't try too hard to avoid it either)?' show that we have a pharisaical approach to God where we want to get as close to the line as we can… without getting punished for sinning.

Why don't we forget the line, and instead draw as close to Jesus as possible… because He loves us. Because He, Himself is so loveable. Because when we do, He gives us the desire (and assistance) to flee anything that will come between us and Him.

After a man with a lusting issue answers the question about sanctification, the next question for him is: 'Does this behaviour bring you closer to other primary people in your life? Are you now closer to your wife, your daughter, your sons, your friend (whose wife you may have just stolen from)?'

When it comes to our husbands' lusting, we need to distinguish between 'will' and 'ability'. Most of our husbands will not have the ability to stop the automatic lusting (or 'noticing') immediately. If they are demonstrating a desire to fight it though, know that in time, and with God's help, the noticing will decrease. And we never know, he may even get to the point where he sees women the way God does – as beloved people. (See more on the solution to lusting in Chapter 17.)

> Initially I believed him when he said he was committed to recovery. He pretended and hid his ongoing addiction for three years. I should have required more than his word. — survey respondent

Compliance Versus Heart Change

Until recently, most of the specialist sex-addiction treatments emphasised cessation of the acting out. While this is important – both for the addict and those being traumatised by this behaviour – many addicts have assumed that the 'acting out' behaviours were all that needed dealing with. Many addicts have taken a legalistic approach to ceasing these behaviours (at least the most obvious ones).

Sexual addiction circles are filled with men who go down their group's checklist every week, put a tick beside each item, and then go out and ogle every teenage girl (or boy) in sight. I've been very triggered, at times, watching them go at it.

This type of 'checklist' or 'negotiated' recovery comes in so far below what God has for a man. He wants nothing short of his son's whole healing. Checklist recovery rarely creates this. Far too often, occasional relapses become frequent ones until these men are further into their addictive behaviour than they had been before they began getting help. At other times, sobriety is maintained, but intimacy doesn't increase. (See more in Chapter 13.)

Pastor Darrell Brazell of New Hope church, in the US, gives a very lucid explanation of why these phenomena are so common. In some of his recovery materials, as well as in one of his free audio files,[137] he discusses the brain science of true recovery. While he agrees that acting out behaviours need to be ceased, core issues also need to be dealt with. How? Through healthy, intimate relationships with God and safe people. This is what causes the brain to heal and true recovery to take place.

What should a wife's reaction be to a man who is only seeking to comply, not to recover? Dr Townsend warns, in *Beyond Boundaries*, that a change of behaviour alone, in the one who has hurt us, indicates we need to maintain our distance.

'Some people think it's unreasonable to expect more from the other person than a change of behaviour. They don't want to be demanding or perfectionistic, so they settle for external modifications rather than internal changes in the other person… Should behaviour changes such as these be enough? I don't want to be a wet blanket, but no. When the person changes behaviour, but you see no evidence that the change is due to a heart-level understanding of how the person impacted you, most likely what you are seeing is compliance. You are not seeing transformation. Compliance is about getting caught and not wanting to get caught again. It does not develop trust.'[138]

Without transformation and the rebuilding of trust we may have a shell of a marriage, but we're not going to have a life-giving, fulfilling relationship (more in Chapter 16).

> My only regret is that I did not separate from him immediately after disclosure. I believe he would have hit bottom sooner. — survey respondent

A Marriage at All Costs?

I was recently at a baby-shower for a single mother in her 20's. She comes from a very broken background: drugs, gangs, abuse, neglect. The father of her baby (and the baby's older brother, then 2) is a drug addict who has raped her, tried to strangle her, threatened her life, tossed her out of a vehicle (with the first child) and made her carry the little one on foot for hours to their home – in the rain.

This man's foster parents are Christians. In fact, mum's a pastor. They are forever pushing this woman and their son to marry.[139] When they started up again at the baby shower, I stood with her in her, 'No!'

Why is it in Christian circles that we see marriage as more important than people? Did Jesus come to this world to save marriages, or the souls of men, women and children?

N, who I support, recently took the risk to tell the principle of the Christian school her girls were interested in attending how her husband would soon be incarcerated for his indecent assaults on the oldest daughter. For her pains, she was treated to a 45 minute lecture. The theme: you can't leave your husband. Forget that there's a court order forbidding him to live with you – God wants you together, so you have no choice!

Wow. So according to this man, God wants their eldest daughter to be told that her stolen innocence is worth nothing? All three girls that their right to live in safety is not as important as a convicted criminal's right to be married (and have access to children)? God wants N to live in terror (breaking the law, we might add) with a man who shows no true remorse for what he's done, and who still lies about it to people and justifies it: showing deep sociopathic tendencies?

Nope. Not Jesus of Nazareth.

And I don't think Jesus says that only those women with felons for husbands get to choose to set a boundary involving leaving. His heart is for the healing of both parties (and their children)… the saving of their souls. The marriage will most likely follow if that happens. However, if the marriage breaks down, I doubt he'll be half as ruffled about it as some Christians.

> I have found sex toys, books, magazines, etc. [I've] gone to our pastor and he told me to pray more!
> — survey respondent

Spiritual Abuse

As for why some clergy turn a blind eye to sexual misconduct (especially of the more discreet variety) and work to convince a woman to stay in a marriage with a known offender, Blankenship states,

'Another issue is that research indicates a high percentage of male clergy are struggling with sexual addiction issues. Without taking their own journey of healing, it is difficult for them to minister to spouses who are in crisis.'[140]

Of course, in some cases the reason is simply ignorance of sexual addiction and partner trauama. This ignorance often leads clergy to side with an addict who is also a master of duplicity and lies.

A survey on spiritual crisis in wives of sex addicts that I conducted in 2015[141] with A Circle of Joy brought forward many stories of mistreatment by church leaders. Some of the respondents shared that they were told:

- You're just paranoid because this was in your first marriage
- You need to lower your expectations
- You need to understand better how grace works
- You aren't allowed to separate

From colleagues in this field I've also heard stories of women being told:

- You women are all just frigid
- Why don't you try and make yourself a bit more attractive
- You need to read Ephesians 5 and start practicing it
- Perhaps if you kept house a bit better…

Thankfully there are a number of organisations working to help clergy come to a better understanding of the nature of sexual addiction and partner trauma – as well as organisations helping clergy caught in their own sexual integrity issues.[142] The result is that while some survey respondents reported spiritual abuse from church leadership, many reported that they had received great support from their pastor and church. The work is begun, but there's still more to go.

In her article, *Did Jesus Heal Marriages?*, A Circle of Joy coach, Christy Kane, writes:

Jesus was concerned with the individual. He did not wait to heal people until their spouse was present. Nor did he tell a wife to read scripture, have more faith, and be more submissive so her husband could be healed. Neither did he blame one person for another's sin or affliction. He had compassion on each individual and healed them, just as he died for each individual.[143]

Those who work in this field will attest to seeing, time and time again, that it's only when the marriage is threatened that many addicts act. If this fact were only better known in our churches, I suspect wives would be afforded a bit more grace when they make hard choices about the marriage.

> But if from there you seek the Lord your God, you will find him if you seek him with all your heart and with all your soul. —Deuteronomy 4:29

Is it Good Enough?

If we have been living for a prolonged period of time with a betrayer who thinks 'Okay, I stopped the porn (etc.), that's good enough,' we are allowed to think again about whether that's 'good enough' for us. If he's looking to lust regularly: we can be sure it's not good enough for the God who wants *him* fully healed, and *us* fully honoured.

Moreover, lusting is really only the symptom of a problem. Is he looking to deal with the underlying problem? Is he trying to move closer to God? To you? Is he actively trying to understand how his sins have impacted you? Is he looking to rebuild trust? Or rather is he remaining emotionally distant, self-absorbed, impatient, etc.?

If he is working on his stuff: excellent. He, himself, should be motivated to tackle the lusting before long. However, don't be shy to put boundaries up related to this and other sexual misconduct while you wait – and follow through on your consequences. In the meantime, you can keep working on your own healing so that the two of you, in time, reach the place where you're ready to start moving beyond boundaries… to borrow the title of one of Dr Townsend's books.[144]

Of course, if he is purposely lusting and not tackling any of the deeper issues, that's a more serious problem. Still, we can work on our own healing. We can seek safe counsel about the relationship, including the counsel of the God who loves us.

Whether we stay in the relationship or not, if we're living with someone who is only complying, it's best to keep strong boundaries in place.

Taking it Further

Read the story of Jonathan and Saul in 1 Samuel 20:27-34.

As you reflect on this story consider that Saul, in killing David, would be breaking his covenant relationship to protect him (David was his armour-bearer). Covenants in old testament times were similar to the vows people take today on marrying: they involved a seven-fold ceremony.

Questions: Do you get the impression that Jonathan sinned against God in going against his father's will and protecting David? (Note: this is certainly how Saul saw it.) Could Jonathan's actions to save David (and even himself in this instance) be seen as a loving act toward his father who would be breaking an important vow to God if he killed David? Do you see any similarities between this story and a situation where a wife leaves a husband intent on infidelity, abuse, anger, etc.?

For more on the topic of submission that is both freeing and challenging, read *God's Panoply* by Anne Hamilton.

> *For Reflection*: Isaiah 62:2-5 and Song of Solomon (optional)

Endnotes

135 Everyman's Battle website, retrieved March, 2015: <http://newlife.com/emb/looking-noticing-and-seeing/>.

136 Struthers, ibid, p. 231.

137 *Brain Science of Sex and Addiction*, <http://bit.ly/13M554u>.

138 Townsend, ibid, 264.

139 They also enable their son's drug habit and abuse of others.

140 Blankenship, p. 88.

141 The Spiritual Crisis survey was conducted in June/July 2015. Some of the responses came out of the follow-up interviews conducted in August/September 2015.

142 See the Resources page at the end of the book.

143 C Kane, 'Did Jesus Heal Marriages?', A Circle of Joy website, accessed, July 2014 <http://bit.ly/1ESkEsK>.

144 *Beyond Boundaries* is also highly recommended reading for those who are considering moving forward again in a relationship formerly broken by betrayal.

My friend from Brisbane scrutinises M for a moment, bows her head and begins to pray. I bow my head, but I'm not following the prayer. I'm writhing in pain and humiliation.

M's done it again: he's sabotaged my special day.

Thank you Abba that A is a relatively imperturbable person, because this is completely humiliating. Not only did I awake this morning to find: no special breakfast, no present, no cake, no... anything to acknowledge my birthday, A found the same. Yes, strangely, A and I, share a birthday and she has come for a visit at this time. She is a friend who deserves honouring, but instead she's going to partake of what is the usual for me.

Well, at least he managed to go out and buy the present I requested him to get her. I wanted it to be a surprise and wasn't sure how to work it into our tour of the local sites. The money my family sent from overseas for my gift has already been spent on groceries apparently. Groceries that didn't include a cake or the ingredients to make one.

Well, I guess it's better than the year that he bought me the pyjamas online...

I look at M who is sitting beside me weeping. He's picked this morning to completely fall apart and ask for prayer ministry.

Somehow, it's always about him.

CHAPTER 13

Intimacy Aversion

Dr Townsend says,

'Partners think that they can explain why their relationship lacks intimacy by the presence of "the problem." They are surprised to find that even when "the problem" goes away, the person with whom they can't connect or find love remains.'[145]

Thus many wives of sex addicts have been disappointed to find that even after their husband has stopped acting out sexually, their marriage relationship is not a fulfilling one where they are cherished and honoured. They still feel they are very much alone in their marriage.

Sex addiction is often referred to as an 'intimacy disorder.' As such, the tendency to avoid intimacy is often 'the problem behind the problem' for many sex addicts. As one respondent to the 2014/2015 Survey stated, 'He is anorexic [avoids intimacy] and in some ways this is more difficult to deal with than SA.'

Intimacy Averse

Intimacy aversion often plays out as control and manipulation of situations and people, for the purpose of maintaining emotional distance. As such, it is like a twisted form of boundaries. Boundaries are designed to keep oneself safe in a relationship with someone who is unhealthy and may cause damage. The sex addict often considers the one trying to draw near, in order to know and offer love, dangerous.

In the majority of cases, it is only the spouse who is on the receiving end of the controlling, though sometimes children are included. To the public, a sex addict will often be striving hard to create and control a 'I'm a great guy' perception. That is how a woman is often wooed into marrying a sex addict. He was such a nice guy until the day after the wedding.[146]

Control and Manipulation

Why does the sex addict avoid intimacy? Why does he control and manipulate? In a nutshell: fear.

Many sex addicts are, at their core, extremely fearful people. In addition to a fear of intimacy, they are afraid of others' opinion of them. These are related notions. The addict often feels that if he were really known he would be disliked and rejected: an idea that is unthinkable to him.

Janice Caudill and Dorit Reichental explained to their audience, at the 2014 IACSAS Redeeming Sexuality and Intimacy conference, that those trying to avoid intimacy keep themselves safe by working hard to avoid being questioned. Because his wife is viewed by him as an object, when she fails to perform the way he wants (e.g., she questions him, disagrees, or suggests he has a flaw), the intimacy-averse addict believes he is justified in punishing her.

The deeper a man (or woman is) in his sex addiction pathology, generally, the stronger his aversion to intimacy. Moreover, he will become more intentional with his control tactics, and use them more frequently.

In the story I just related, M was not intentionally trying to to ruin my birthday, he was mostly just being self-obsessed and self-pitying. This type of behaviour has always just happened to come out most particularly on days such as my birthday, our anniversary, Christmas, Valentine's and other times where he might be expected to draw nearer to me or honour me. Sabotaging such days for his spouse is a common intimacy aversion technique.

At the far end of the sex addiction spectrum, we may find men/women who are incredibly intentional in their sabotaging of special days. They may even state that intention before or during the event. I think of a SA relative who would boast, each year, about not buying his wife a Christmas gift (something he never did in 20 years of marriage).

In cases, such as this, where the aversion behaviours are this glaring and wounding, women most definitely need to establish boundaries (see Chapter 7). They would also be well-advised to seek healing for the damage that comes naturally when living with such a broken individual.

To love at all is to be vulnerable. Love anything, and your heart will be wrung and possibly broken. If you want to be sure of keeping your heart intact you must give your heart to no one, not even an animal. Wrap it carefully around with hobbies and little luxuries, avoid all entanglements. Lock it up safely in the casket of your selfishness. And in that casket, safe, dark, motionless, airless, it will not change, it will not be broken. It will become unbreakable, impenetrable and irredeemable. The only place outside of heaven where you can be perfectly safe from the dangers of love is hell.

— CS Lewis

Control Tactics

Besides sabotaging special days, intimacy-aversion causes the sex addict to make frequent use of the 12 techniques listed in the chart on the next page. The goal? Control his spouse and avoid intimacy.

Let's take a look at a few of the key techniques Caudill and Reichental expounded on in their joint conference presentation.

- **Withholding Love** – According to the two women, someone who is intimacy averse will 'treat expressions of love as a commodity to control the level of intimacy in the relationship. He rarely initiates or responds to requests for verbal or nonverbal expressions of love.'

- **Withholding Praise** – Those who are intimacy averse tend to have a negative narrative about their spouse going on in their head, and so are more likely to see only the negative. When they do praise, it is often paired with criticism, i.e., it's a back-handed compliment.
- **Busyness as a Barrier** – The sex addict will often keep himself over-busy in order to avoid intimacy. This also helps him create and maintain his 'great guy', public image.
- **Anger** – A sex addict may use verbal or non-verbal expressions of anger to sabotage an emotional connection with his wife. Another tactic is to manipulate her into an expression of anger, so that she will not initiate a connection.
- **Silence** – This technique ranges from abrupt changes of subject to zero verbal response. Alternatively, all responses may be dismissive or hostile. A partner's retaliatory silent treatment only serves to help her intimacy-averse spouse reach his goal faster.

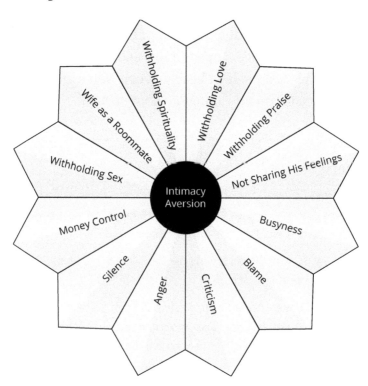

Withholding Sex

The control method of 'withholding sex' is so common with sex addicts, who are active in their addiction, that it is worth looking at this phenomenon a bit closer.[147]

As one of the most intimate acts a human being can engage in, sex with one's spouse is obviously perceived as being highly dangerous to the intimacy averse. Many of the withholding and sabotaging techniques work to make his partner less keen to engage in sex with him. However if these don't work, there are other ways to avoid sex such as non-initiation (repeated), excuses around health/fatigue, overindulging in alcohol (or claiming to have overindulged), claims it will hurt his recovery, etc.[148] Of course, many sex addicts appear to have a low libido… but in reality have a very active sex life with porn, etc.

When a sex addict does engage in sex with his partner, explain Caudill and Reichental, it is predominantly objectifying/narcissistic sex. This is sex where the partner is treated more as an object. The addict will avoid eye contact, nurturing communication and emotional contact. He will also often fantasise during sex. Moreover, he will in many cases, leave the partner when finished… either emotionally, physically or both.

Such underwhelming sexual experiences (for the healthy partner) may serve to stop her from initiating, or may at least cause her to initiate less frequently.

The Stats

There have been no academic studies done to date on intimacy aversion; however, IACSAS president, Richard Blankenship, feels that every sex addict exhibits these behaviours to one degree or another.

As part of the 2014/2015 Survey of Wives of Sex Addicts, I asked the respondents about whether periods of abstinence had been initiated by their husbands and gave them a chance to express any concerns they had about that. Avoiding sexual intimacy is, of course, one of the many areas where intimacy aversion is wounding women.

25% of the respondents said their husband had initiated a period of abstinence in the marriage.[149] Of these respondents, 46% said the effect on *their healing* was negative to highly negative (23% listed the effect as neutral). 46% also said the effect of sexual intimacy avoidance on *their marriage* was negative to highly negative (28% listed it as neutral).

Effects on the Partner

Below are some of the heart-rending responses women gave about their husband's lack of sexual interest in them.

- 'I do not feel honoured or cherished.'
- 'He made it obvious he didn't need me which really hurt.'
- 'The biggest blow to my self-esteem ever.'
- 'It is pushing us even further apart.'
- 'I hate it.'
- 'He would not initiate with me… it made me feel very insecure.'
- 'I felt rejected and unwanted.'
- 'He blamed me for… rendering him impotent.'
- 'He said I had nothing to offer him and he owed me even less.'
- 'He has not touched me in 15 years. I am living a lie.'

For a time, say Caudill and Reichental, a wife will try harder to please her husband, but after repeated failed attempts to meet his unrealistic and ever-changing expectations, she will give up. She will doubt herself, shut down emotionally – and often sexually – as a protective mechanism.

An example of this is seen in the survey response of one wife who said, 'He was trying to use it [abstinence] to punish me… until he realised I didn't care.' This is tragic, because there was probably a time when she did care. However, she's had to shut down in order to avoid the pain of rejection and intimacy deprivation.

Some therapists see this kind of response in the wife as 'intimacy anorexia', or 'intimacy aversion' as well. Others call it 'reactive anorexia'. However, more and more this protective response, on the part of the partner, is being seen as normal, natural, and thus, not in need of a label. At the time of writing, Richard Blankenship was in the process of authoring an article making this point.

Whatever the label (preferably none) their response is given, there are more options for women than just shutting down. These will be discussed at the end of the chapter.

Fear of Intimacy: What's Behind It?

Sexual trauma, seeing his father neglect his mother, attachment issues with either parent (but particularly the opposite gender parent) are considered by Caudill and Reichental to be the key causes of intimacy aversion tendencies. Not surprisingly, they are also some of the key issues behind sexual addiction in general. As professionals, the women often see improvement in the intimacy aversion when these underlying issues are treated.

According to Caudill and Reichental, if left untreated, intimacy aversion will not resolve. Moreover, it may even prevent the sexual addiction from resolving. By the 'sexual addiciton' the women clearly are referring to the 'acting out' side of the addiction.

The women also argue that typical recovery programmes for sex addicts exacerbate intimacy issues. Part of the problem, they state, is that these programmes put too much emphasis on behavioural changes (see more in Chapter 12). Such change, the women feel, should be seen as the end goal, the result of the more fundamental healing and growth that must be the starting point.

'He might be the hero of his recovery group,' Reichental says, 'however traditional treatment, with its "you do your work/I'll do mine" philosophy, fosters sobriety, but reinforces a lack of emotional connection in the traumatised relationship.'[150]

For those looking to understand more about how to grow in the ability to connect emotionally, I recommend Dr Townsend's *Loving People: How to Love and Be Loved*. Other useful reading would be Shepherd's House's, *The Life Model*. The chapter on different types of relational bonds may be particularly enlightening for a man who believes he can keep himself safe by avoiding intimacy.

The Shepherd House authors write:

'There are two essentially different and incompatible types of bonds [between people]– one based on fear and the other on love. Fear bonds are formed around avoiding negative feelings and pain. Love bonds are formed around desire, joy and seeking to be with people who are important to us. Fear bonds energise people to avoid pain – like rejection, fear, shame, humiliation, abandonment, guilt or even physical abuse. Love bonds motivate people to live in truth, closeness, joy, peace, perseverance, kindness and authentic giving… when the shared bond is fear, anxiety builds as the time approaches to be together.[151]

In *The Life Model*, the authors discuss how to turn fear bonds into love bonds. Moreover, Shepherd House has produced a booklet on an excellent prayer ministry technique for helping resolve the past trauma that may make people intimacy averse. This booklet, *Share Immanuel* could go a long way to helping our sex addicts tackle their deeper issues around intimacy.

Couple's Therapy

It's not uncommon to find couples, where one partner is intimacy averse, living more as roommates, or business partners, than as a married couple.

Reichental, who is one of the top marriage counsellors in the US specialising in sexual addiction, uses Imago exercises and emotionally-focused couple therapy (EFCT) with her clients.

Imago is based on techniques such as dialogue mirroring. Reichental says she recommends couples do Imago exercises, dialoguing about feelings, three night's per week for 15 minutes. A therapist trained in Imago techniques can help them get started.

EFCT, she states, should be the next step, at about six months into treatment. This particular therapy focuses on 'helping people become aware of and express their emotions, learn to tolerate and regulate them, reflect on them to make sense of them, and transform them.'[152]

The Limitations of Couple's Therapy

As always, with therapy, there are various factors that contribute to its success.

29% of respondents to the 2014/2015 Survey said they felt they had achieved positive results[153] from either couples' counselling or couples' specialist therapy. 57%, however, said they experienced negative results. Written responses regarding the results ranged from 'life-changing' to 'catastrophic'.

The number one issue cited for negative results was the husband. Problems listed were that he was not engaged, did not follow through, or that he outright lied to the counsellor.

The second major issue cited was the therapist. Concerns ranged from a lack of understanding of sexual addiction and the trauma response in partners to victim-blaming or suggesting the couple use porn together.

Let's remember we can always leave a bad counsellor and try again. Said one American survey respondent:

'[Our] first CSAT [certified sex-addiction therapist] was victim-blaming and didn't help my husband at all to understand the impact on me. Rather, he assisted him to minimise the seriousness of what he had done. [Our] current counsellor uses Emotionally Focused

Therapy which is gradually helping my husband to address severe emotional anorexia [intimacy aversion] and re-learn how to relate as a couple.'

So, in a perfect world, we find a marriage counsellor who is Imago and EFT certified[154] and also certified with IACSAS. That's the Christmas shopping list. Those in Australia or New Zealand, may have to settle for less, but hopefully not much less.[155]

Several survey respondents mentioned that they felt they had entered couple's therapy too early. They sensed that their individual therapy (including trauma therapy for the wife) should have been given more time before there was a move into couple's work. While this may be true, keep in mind that couple's therapy may very well be one of the key components of addressing intimacy issues. Having her husband address these issues, could equally prove very healing to his wife.

Other Options

With enough diligent searching, and possibly some 'trial and error', it is usually possible to find good couple's therapy. However, therapy is only one piece of this puzzle. According to the therapist-authors of *The Life Model*:

'Even though therapy can help people face the places that are stuck in their lives, it alone will not supply the power to get them unstuck. A family and a community need to supply some of the power. That is where people are supposed to find out who they are, and where they are supposed to find help in getting unstuck. It is where they should receive life.'[156]

The authors go on to add that when natural family is unable to provide this, 'God's plan [is] to bring spiritual family members into a person's life.'

Which brings us nicely back around to the source of all healing.

God does not want us to become embittered through lack of healthy emotional connection. God desires to nourish and nurture us. He desires us to be in life-giving relationships. Call on him as Jehovah-Jireh: the Lord who Provides.

If we choose to stay with a sex addict who continues to avoid intimacy, remember, there are also boundaries. For myself, I introduced a strange one into our relationship. After eight years of being the initiator of sex, more than 90% of the time, I said I would not initiate sex again. It worked to M's advantage for awhile (mine too, actually, as I needed some space). However, as he started to recover – not just from his addiction, but also from his fears and emotional disconnectedness – this boundary has helped him to 'step up' and take risks.

And as Dr Townsend says,

'Great relationships are fulfilling. Great relationships involve risk. You can't have the first without the second. Great relationships require that you be open to taking risks – risks of being misunderstood, of alienation, of someone being hurt by you as well. It doesn't mean relationships aren't worth the risks, for the good ones are. It is simply the price of the course. No pain, no gain.'[157]

May our intimacy averse husbands come to understand this.

Taking it Further

What do we do with our own sexual energy when our husband is rejecting us in the bedroom? The pain and sorrow we are facing may be naturally lowering our libido, but when it is making itself felt, we need to turn to God and offer it to Him.

Other coping techniques include making time for intimacy with friends and family, extra exercise, and projects which are intellectually stimulating.

It's important to practice extra good boundaries with other men during this time, to avoid falling into an affair. For the same reason, and to avoid an unhealthy addiction of our own, we may choose to avoid romance literature at this time.

According to a recent study, 15% of Christian women are viewing pornography monthly.[158] It's difficult to say if this statstic includes reading erotica and visiting chat rooms – some of the most common ways women act out sexually. In any case, let's not become part of the statistic. Help is available if we are willing to reach out.

For *Reflection*: Psalm 91:9-16

Endnotes

145   Cloud and Townsend, ibid.

146   In some cases the the intimacy averse partner defers, explains Caudill & Reichental, until the birth of the first child.

147   There are, of course, other reasons why a sex addict may not iniate sex with his wife, including SA-induced impotence and low libido. Thanks to Richard Blankenship for this addition.

148   Thank you to the 2014/2015 Survey of Wives of Sex Addicts respondents for these examples.

149   A few of the respondents mentioned the abstinence was under the direction of a counsellor.

150   Caudill & Reichental

151   *The Life Model, Living From the Heart Jesus Gave You*, eds. JG Friesen, EJ Wilder, AM Berling, R Kopecke, M Pool, Shepherd's House, 2013, p. 59.

152   Emotion-Focused Therapy Clinic, <http://www.emotionfocusedclinic.org/whatis.htm>.

153   I have listed the ending of the marriage with the positive results where the wife stated she felt this was a positive outcome.

154   The current online list mentions one practitioner in Australia.

155   While not thereapists, there is a couple in the US who do couple's coaching for those with intimacy aversion and attachment issues: Steve and Kristie Farnworth of Pathway to Intimacy.

156   Friesen et al, ibid, p. 10.

157   Townsend, ibid, p. 10.

'I heard a voice just as I woke up say, "gods who are deceitful should be drowned!"'

'What? That's horrible... whose voice?'

'Actually, it was kind of like mine. And it gets worse. As I was going to sleep, I found myself thinking "I should drown him." *Him*, was definitely God. I was thinking before that about times God has let me down.'

'Oh wow.'

'I know. It scared me, that's not like me to think something like that. There's obviously a spiritual problem here.'

CHAPTER 14

Our Battle

Nightmares so horrendous they would make a sex offender blanch. That was my first indication that perhaps, along with the emotional and psychological issues of addiction, we were looking at spiritual problems as well.

These nightmares weren't occasional either. At the beginning of recovery, M had nightmares where he was sex offending multiples times per week – other nights he was just being unfaithful (almost a relief in comparison).

As former sex addict and (current) counsellor, Charles Finck says, when you're dealing with sex addiction, you're always looking at a spiritual issue as well. 'Sex addiction opens up the person wide enough for Satan to drive a Mac [i.e., 'transport'] truck in and start unloading.'[159]

But how do we know for sure there's a spiritual problem? What do we do if we are sure?

> A people who fear and refuse to embrace authentic spiritual reality will therefore be embraced by sexual addiction and effectively worship sexual desire – much as other, ancient pagans. — Gordon Dalbey

Two Camps

In the Christian world there are many opinions about the dark side of the spiritual realm. Christians tend, however, to fit in one of two camps. The first is the, 'we don't want to know about it' camp. The second are the spiritual commandos who are ready to shoot first and ask questions (of their Leader) later.

In the first camp we find the people who are convinced that all issues around character (strengths or defects) are psychological. Most will admit, however, that those psychological issues may affect a person's spirit as well.

These folks are often uncomfortable with the fact that the spiritual side of life is non-quantifiable. We pray… and many times we don't see anything happen. Or maybe something does happen, but not *when* we think it should, or *the way* we think it should and… maybe it was the change in diet. Most spiritual ministry rubs our methodical, Western worldview the wrong way.

Then there's the second camp. Here you get, 'all issues are spiritual… however they may affect a person's psyche.' This side are known for finding a beloved formula and applying it to every person and situation. They too frequently over-promise (this is guaranteed to solve the problem), and if they under-deliver: 'it was your lack of faith'.

Interestingly, if we combine these two ideas, we come up with something that's started to make a lot of sense to me (and others): any major issue will have both a psychological and spiritual component to it. Both need to be dealt with. Sometimes dealing with one takes care of the other, but not always.

Dreams

A well-known American Christian counsellor and author, whose work I admire for the most part, recently wrote that dreams of sexual betrayal are innocuous.

Admittedly, after years of living through the nightmare, of a husband having nightmares, she'd hit one of my sore points.

To me, when we are talking about a sex addict having these kinds of dreams, they are not innocuous. Most such dreams stem from past or present sin – making them at the very least, a symptom of a disease that needs treating.

In *Every Man's Battle*, Steve Arterburn and Fred Stoeker discuss the fact that the techniques men use to fight their addiction in real life will, in time, become techniques they use in their dreams. Says Stoeker: 'You'll know you're nearing victory when, even in the freedom of your dream state, your subconscious mind still chooses purity.'[160]

M, found this to be true… it was just slow to become the norm.

As you can imagine, there was a lot of praying, on both our parts, about these dreams. After awhile we began to see a pattern in them. Each dream focused on a different sin M had committed as part of his addiction… or outside of his addiction. Each dream was an opportunity to repent of a sin.

Now some will argue that since M was a Christian, he'd repented of these sins already. Having done so, Jesus had forgiven him so it must be all over. Why would he have to repent again?

I'm not able to comment on any case but this one, but I can say with certainty that M had never repented specifically for any of these sins until he went into recovery. When he started repenting in early recovery, it wasn't, originally, with deep contrition. Reliving these sins in his dreams, helped him connect emotionally, on waking, with what he'd done. Repentance was then with true remorse.

Of course, this process was extremely painful for me. New dreams each night of old girlfriends, specific porn used, friends and family members he'd lusted after in various ways were triggering and painful. However, God helped me cope by running me through the same process.

Yup… I was also getting dreams where I was reliving sins of my past. In the dreams I could more readily identify the sin and the harm it had done others. One night it was about neglecting my children's needs while we were at a party. Another, it was about standing by and watching a friend come to erroneous spiritual conclusions – without challenging her in love (though the Holy Spirit was elbowing me in the ribs to do so).

For about six months, M and I were regularly having dreams that gave us an opportunity to see where we'd sinned, discuss it with God and repent in a heartfelt manner.

I'd like to say that at the end of the six months: presto, the dreams vanished, but that wasn't the case. However, by that time M had really begun to grow and change. He was able increasingly to be the same person in his dreams that he was in the daytime: a man fighting a battle against selfishness, false refuges and lust.

Spiritual warfare and ministry don't come with the nice, neat 'cause and effect' we Western-world thinkers like to see. That's why I can only guess that this first set of experiences – understanding and repenting with contrition – were a necessary step before some of the bigger spiritual issues could be dealt with. Those bigger spiritual issues included those sex offender dreams.

> For our struggle is not against flesh and blood, but against the rulers, against the authorities, against the powers of this dark world and against the spiritual forces of evil in the heavenly realms. —Ephesians 6:12

Battle Gear

M had never been comfortable with the idea of spiritual warfare. However, one of his initial counsellors was. In fact, G was perhaps too comfortable with it. G prayed M through the process of cutting ties with all his former sexual partners. This is very common in prayer ministry and is a good thing for both the betrayer and the wife to do. Moreover, it's not likely to have any negative spiritual repercussions.[161]

So while G showed wisdom in some aspects of spiritual warfare, he also serves as a good example of how formulaic approaches can go wrong. G did prison ministry with sex offenders. There was one inmate who was clearly demon-possessed. On three occasions, G went in, spoke to the demon, bound and cast it out. Each time, the deliverance lasted only hours.

Now, this is a common method of delivering someone possessed by a demon. It seems to follow the model Jesus gave the disciples. Why didn't it work?

The spiritual realm is truly beyond us humans. That's why we must tread carefully and only by the direction of the Spirit. I suspect G's heart was in the right place… but perhaps his ear wasn't.

Now, I have to admit that having come to the conclusion that all sex addicts have some degree of spiritual affliction, M and I tried the 'bind and cast' method early in recovery. We tried getting rid of a spirit of perversion, lust etc. We were going prayerfully, trying to discern which spirits might need tackling. There were no observable results from this exercise. Maybe G wasn't the only one with his ear in the wrong place.

Fortunately, we're a little better at hearing the leading of the Holy Spirit these days than we were then. And I'm not saying we're brilliant at it yet. However, we've got four more years of practicing conversational prayer with God,[162] and looking back, it's pretty clear to me we were just fumbling around with no real clue as to what we were doing. I realise now, that when I'm in a traumatised state: I have serious difficulties hearing the Holy Spirit and discerning what He's saying to me.

Now that I'm no longer in 'crisis' mode, I'm at least better at realising, 'Wow, I don't have a clue what to do'. So is M. We're also wise enough now to drop the subject until our Abba *gives* us a clue. Sometimes he leads us directly (through something like a scripture passage/dream combination). Sometimes it's through experienced prayer ministers confirming what God has already put in our hearts. Sometimes our small prayer group gives direction.

One of the books that M first found helpful on his journey into spiritual warfare was *No Small Snakes* by Gordon Dalbey. Dalbey stresses repeatedly that one should not move ahead with spiritual warfare without direction from the Holy Spirit. He also talks about the benefits of fasting regularly when one feels called to be tackling spiritual problems. This not only puts us in a position to tackle more kinds of issues ('This kind can come out only by prayer and fasting', Mark 9:29), but also tends to make most of us more attuned to the voice of the Spirit.

Of course, it's not like M and I became mighty prayer warriors after reading this book, ready to tackle all the spiritual issues facing us. Not long after finishing it, M was feeling frustrated for the struggles of a brother for whom he was an accountability partner. Emboldened by his new knowledge of spiritual warfare, he prayed for the binding of the spirit of same-sex attraction in this man's life, and for it to be cast out. The result: that night M had his first ever homosexual dream.

Clearly we weren't quite there yet.

> He is somewhat verbally abusive and says bizarre things that seem evil and not of a man who says he's changed... I've had to learn my battle is not with my husband but with the enemy who seeks to destroy anything that might further the Lord's kingdom and His truth.
>
> — survey respondent

Tackling the Generational

As I've already stated, M has struggled with two different kinds of sex dreams. Most commonly his dreams have a direct and fairly obvious link to his past sin. However, there has been another type: one where the dreams have an obvious twist of evil to them. Most of these are dreams I summarise as his 'sex offender' dreams.

Now, while M had never done, in real life, the things he was doing in these dreams, his grandfather had. His sisters were victimised as a result. M rarely shared the details of these dreams, but what he did share was enough to leave me terrified and traumatised. He himself was traumatised. They were becoming the number one biggest strain on our relationship at one point.

We were very blessed, though, to have a friend who is a long-time prayer minister. One day I confided to her about the issue and she took it away and prayed about it. She came back after awhile and talked about the fact that the bible shows us a precedent for a person repenting of a sin on behalf of their family. Since we knew this particular sin was in the family line, she recommended M try this.

M prayed this prayer one time, approximately two years ago from the time of this writing. Prior to that, he'd had approximately one to two dreams of this nature every week for over three years. Since that time he's had three dreams with a hint of the old theme, but nothing that displayed anything like the level of evil in the previous dreams.

Three dreams in the past two years. Thank God for sending us the right person with the right information – and I suspect, at the right time.

God wants us to be free. If you suspect that there are generational issues at work in your life, or your husband's, ask Him to direct you to those who can help. Ask if you should be repenting on behalf of your family. Ask about whether you need prayer to break generational ties.

There may be advance work that needs to be done before prayer ministry for generational issues. God alone knows. Fortunately for us: He's on our side. Ask him to lead the way.

In His Time

Today M has the occasional dream with a female demon/goddess figure. I've even had dreams on a couple of occasions about M and spirits that pose as women. These are very creepy for M and a reminder that the spiritual issues are progressing, but they're not gone yet.

He also used to struggle with falling asleep at inappropriate times: most commonly during a bible- or Christian-book study, as well as during serious, emotional conversations. This may have been a problem with an outside spirit or what is referred to as a 'sleeping spirit' – a problem in his own spirit. I believe this was overcome by M doing a lot of the ground work in spiritual and emotional growth. Next, those gifted in prayer ministry came on the scene to take him the next part of the way. Finally, it was back to more growth on M's part again until the issue gradually resolved.

It's tempting to get impatient and just start claiming authority over unseen forces and commanding them to back off. But, I've come to see that a lot of spiritual warfare is simply praying and waiting for God to reveal things by his Spirit. Most of the time, it's not specific spiritual culprits He reveals, but lies we have believed, sins we have committed, judgements we have made, and false refuges and mental constructs we have hidden in.

Once we repent of such things and ask to be transformed in such a way that we can leave them behind, I suspect we are a big step closer to deliverance. Who knows, maybe our baggage is the infrastructure the enemy needs to maintain a bothersome presence in our lives, and once it is removed, we can ask God to dismiss any spiritual forces that may be in operation.

From what I've witnessed so far, deliverance of this type doesn't require us to address spirits, name them, personally try to grapple with them – or any of these other dramatic, but possibly dangerous methods that some employ. Of course, God may direct some of His children to this type of interaction. I don't mind that I'm not one of them.

When Help is Unwanted

There are, of course, a number of sex addicts, betrayers, etc. who want nothing to do with repentance, deliverance or prayer ministry of any kind. Sometimes the wife is certain, though, that there are powerful spirits involved with her husband and they are playing havoc with the family.

My daughter, as a toddler, on a couple of occasions saw another man in our room with us who frightened her. I have read almost this exact same story from the wife of another sex addict. Husbands living a life of deception leave their families vulnerable.

Obviously the first answer is our own prayers for our children's (and our own) safety from spiritual defilement and attack. We can get backup on this as well. Secondly, we can ask God how best to pray for our husbands. Let's not assume He wants us taking on the spirits that affect him, this very moment.

If you are not (yet) a person who hears much from God, I'd recommend the book *Whispers of My Abba*, by David Tackle.[163] This book makes conversational prayer readily understandable and non-intimidating. Do keep in mind that, like myself, you may find it harder to hear and discern the Spirit in times of high emotion and stress. This is where your support people can be invaluable.

Also, please be aware that at a certain point, some sex addicts, betrayers and offenders hit levels of evil that, some hypothesise, gives them spiritual power. I became aware of this phenomenon only recently: as I was ministering to two different women, one in Australia, one in New Zealand, both of whom are the wives of sex offenders.

Though both are intelligent, Christian women, I was shocked to see them being so easily manipulated by their respective husbands. Both men had their wives convinced that they (the men) were innocent victims – that even the wives were more culpable for their injuries than they were.

With permission I took this to my prayer group. One of the women in the group came back quickly to say she did not believe either woman was gullible, or even easily manipulated. Quoting the theories of Ted Peters in *Sin: Radical Evil in Soul and Society*[164] she explained that once a person descends to level five in the following list, they seem to have incredible spiritual power to convince everyone – including the victim – that they are the innocent party. The table, which details the path from least to greatest evil, runs as such:

1. Anxiety
2. "Unfaith" (failure to trust God)
3. Pride
4. Concupiscence (coveting power)
5. Self-justification and scapegoating
6. Cruelty
7. Blasphemy, including reversal of symbols

Both husbands had definitely reached level five, and I suspect one was all the way at seven (where he calls evil, 'good' and good, 'evil'). I would add that one of the reasons these men are so convincing is that they absolutely believe, themselves, that they are innocent. In other words, their sin has made them delusional.

It is so important that we pray for women like these two wives. Pray that God puts his armour on them and that they are able to be alert and stand firm! (Ephesians 6).

I challenged both of these women to also pray for themselves, that they would see only God's truth in regards to their husbands. I began to pray this for myself as well. Within a week, one of the women and I got back together and compared notes. Not only was *she* better identifying her husband's lies, and standing firm against them, but *I* too caught M in a lie. For my part, I'm convinced it was praying specifically about protection from our husbands' delusions that made the difference.

> [I] realised that the suicidal thoughts were from the devil and so I repented to God and told them to go in Jesus' name and they haven't come back.
>
> — survey respondent

Easily Overlooked

It's very easy for us to get caught up in our husband's spiritual state: his sin, his level of repentance, his spiritual baggage. However, let's not kid ourselves. Sex addicts/betrayers aren't the only ones with baggage: we all potentially have it. Moreover, if we didn't have any before our husband's sexual addiction, there's a good possibility we've contracted from him what Gordon Dalbey calls, an STD – spiritually transmitted disease.[165]

Abba recently made this frighteningly clear to me. Remember the exchange at the beginning of this chapter? Were you clear on who was saying what?

I admit, I left it vague. But did you think M was the one having his thoughts invaded so that he was thinking blasphemous things?

It was me actually. He's the one responding in disbelief.

While writing this book, I felt the Father call me to do a few days of very deep grieving. As He was leading the way, I was rather surprised to find that the last day he lead me to grieve the times I felt He had disappointed me. Actually, to be honest, I'd felt at times that He'd ripped me off and deceived me. That day, I relived probably every negative emotion I'd felt about Him with terrifying force. Outside an incredible storm was raging.

That night, the events in that first story transpired. Was I scared? Yes... and very confused.

Thankfully I had my prayer minister friend (and the support of M and my prayer group) to help me through.

I wish I could tell you what exactly it was about, but I can't. Was Abba getting rid of a spirit that had held me for years? Was their an opportunistic spirit trying to gain entry? I don't know, but that's definitely the closest attack I have ever encountered (as far as I'm aware), and I don't want to go through anything like it again.

The only thing I'm certain of is that God wanted me to share that experience in this book. Perhaps like me, you need reminding that our husbands aren't necessarily the only ones in the family who need deliverance.

Taking It Further

There are many different theories on how to deal with evil spiritual forces that may be oppressing us and our families. Most agree on the the following:

- Jesus' power is needed
- Prayer Is needed and sometimes fasting along with prayer
- God's guidance/revelation is needed because this is His specialty realm, not ours
- Repentance, and sometimes renunciation, of sins and sinful habits may be needed (as per what the Holy Spirit reveals... not other people's guesses).

And while it is tempting to look for a checklist or formula to apply to spiritual warfare or delivery, increasingly there are those who are stating there is no 'quick fix'. We need to trust in God's timing and accept that there may be a process involved that centres on the afflicted drawing increasingly close to God and surrendering to Him, before spiritual forces can be dismissed.

As regards the spiritual, psychological and/or physiological aspects of your husband's addiction, can you be at peace with the idea that God may choose not to instantly heal him? Are you open to a miraculous healing all the same? Can you see why it might not be in your husband's best interests to receive instant freedom from his addiction and other spiritual afflictions?

Have you asked God to cut you off from spiritual forces your husband may have allowed into your family? Infidelity doesn't just open the sinful partner to spiritual attack, but his whole family – particularly his wife (through sexual relations).

For Reflection: Romans 8:38-39

Follow-up reading: Pure Sex: The Spirituality of Desire by Gordon Dalbey

Endnotes

158 2014 Pornography Survey and Statistics. Proven Men Ministries. Accessed September 3, 2015, <http://www.provenmen.org/2014pornsurvey/> .

159 C Fink, Sexual Addiction, Elijah House Ministries video, date unknown.

160 S Arterburn and F Stoeker. *Every Man's Battle: Every Man's Guide to Winning the War on Sexual Temptation One Victory at a Time* (The Every Man Series), ebook, p. 206.

161 That said, I have learned to make no assumptions. Always ask God if it's all right to do anything in the spiritual realm: however innocuous seeming.

162 See more on conversational prayer in the section 'When Help is Unwanted'.

163 Kingdom Formation Ministries, 2013.

164 Eerdmans 1994, also, *GOD—The World's Future*, Fortress 2000, Chapter 5. http://www.plts.edu/docs/ite_sin.pdf

165 Dalbey, ibid, p. 281.

'Jesus: where were you when M told me my breasts were a turn off?'

I've been practicing Immanuel Prayer, a form of theophostic prayer, for some time now. I've asked Jesus to return with me to all kinds of painful situations and show me where he was at that time. But I know I've been avoiding this one: the incident whose pain pushed me over the edge.

Today, my heart is burning with the pain of it again, though it's been many months since I felt even passively suicidal.

I've asked the question, with faith I'll get an answer – but maybe not a lot of faith. I'm caught off guard when the answer comes to me within hours: that night before going to sleep.

~ . ~

I visualise myself lying on the ground, stomach downward, but my head turned to one side. There's an enormous cast-iron safe on me. It's been dropped out of the sky on to me and has almost killed me. There's blood trickling out of my mouth, my nose. I know my lungs have been crushed and as I try to breathe I can feel the gurgling of blood. It hurts too much to continue.

My vision is blurred, but I notice the hazy outline of a face just beyond mine. It's Jesus. He's lying beside me on the ground and he's staring intently into my eyes. I want to die, but he's willing me to live.

'Take a breath, please, for me.'

He is so beautiful, and his compassion is compelling. I take one. I don't want to, but his love and passion for me gives me the strength to do it. Then he asks me to take another one. Then again.

I can feel him pouring the will to live into me.
It's the only thing keeping me going.

I realise that if one of my children were on the point of death, this is what I'd be doing. I'd be coaxing them to live. I'd be pouring out my heart, though I probably would not understand their pain. But, Jesus understands mine. I can sense that he's been here.

I continue to return his intense stare. I can't even feel the pressure of the safe any more. I'm so captivated by his eyes, by his intensity.

Suddenly I'm rejoicing in my spirit. What does it matter that my husband rejects me. In comparison to Jesus' love... what is that?

My mouth turns up and I continue to breathe. I sense that some day, his mantra will change from 'Breathe,' to, 'Love. Forgive.'

Some day is fine. For now it's just, 'breathe'.

CHAPTER 15

Forgiveness

The wife of an unfaithful man is often put under incredible pressure to forgive her husband. Sometimes she even puts this pressure on herself.

I've come to realise that there is a lot of erroneous thinking in Christian circles around forgiveness. When it comes to betrayal, 'forgive and forget' is not only unwise, it's impossible. Nevertheless, it's often what is demanded of a wife.

The forgiveness journey is not going to look the same for any two women. However, there are some general principles that we can follow that will assist us along the way. Likewise there are some common pitfalls that are best avoided, so the process doesn't get derailed.

> To magically state that forgiveness is simple and takes place in an instant is to drive the victim deeper into devastation and anger towards God.
>
> — Richard Blankenship

Quick Forgiveness

Jason and Shelley Martinkus tell the story of Shelly's original 'quick forgiveness' of Jason – for his betrayal of her.

Says Shelly,

'I felt pressure from a biblical standpoint… but for me there was something unhealthy because I just saw this [our relationship] as an unhealthy situation and I wanted to get out of it by forgiving really quick. I realise that I did not want to feel everything… the full gravity of our situation – and I used forgiveness as more of a band-aid to almost by-pass a lot of the grieving process. "I'm gonna forgive you. Let's move on. You don't want to talk about it any more. Great! I don't either."' [166]

Shelley's round of quick forgiveness was done within three days of Jason's first 'disclosure' (he was still hiding most of his story at this time). After this she admits that she put pressure on herself not to discuss his betrayal, but instead to just 'forgive and forget.'

Jason says, 'That felt like a good deal for me… What that did was enable me to keep more secrets, and it enabled you [Shelley] to not have to feel the pain… I pawned it off on you to make it right.' [167]

Shelley says she was in denial for the next nine months, just coping with work and other things. It was only when she went away on a trip with a friend that she took a moment to grasp what had happened to her. That was when she realised she was bitter.

In the interim Jason and Shelley did things that made it look like their relationship was doing well. However, both state that the relationship was actually 'crappy' during this period.

They realise now that this kind of quick forgiveness is not healthy. 'There was no healing, no grieving, no honesty.' says Jason. 'No full disclosure,' adds Shelley.

> We are further apart than before. All because he says, "Change takes time, be patient, boundaries and consequences are not biblical, only God gives consequences. I've asked forgiveness from God and I am forgiven so you must forgive me too." [To him] forgiveness = no consequences. — survey respondent

Forgive and Forget

Richard Blankenship has some excellent thoughts on forgiveness in *Spouses of Sex Addicts*. On the topic of 'forgive and forget' he says:

Addicts have ridiculed their spouses by assuming that forgiveness means that they shouldn't have to experience consequences, and things should return to normal upon confession of their addiction.[168]

One of the unavoidable consequences for the addict: his wife will likely be traumatised and will display some of the strange behaviours of traumatised people. At the very least she should be angry, sorrowful, and have questions. If she's not exhibiting these things: she's probably still in shock. Either that or she's trying to repress a tidal wave of painful emotions because she's been told she has to.

A wise husband will – rather than telling his wife, 'forgive and forget' – encourage her at this time to process the pain. He will lead her into the grieving process if necessary and sit with her in it. Forgiveness and trust will come about naturally as part of this… in time.

The chances of this scenario coming to pass, I admit, are slim. Most sex addicts lack the necessary level of maturity to offer their wives this much love and support. Thus we are usually left to fumble our way toward health – including forgiveness – on our own, or supported by others outside the marriage relationship.

While it's rare to find a husband willing to help us on our journey to forgiveness, it's, sadly, far too common to find one hijacking the process. How? By insisting we forgive: now! Not only forgive, but forgive and forget so that things 'go back to normal'. Normal, in the addict's mind generally includes his wife not exhibiting any of her pain, buying his lies and excuses and trusting him again – while he acts out.

This would, indeed, be very convenient for the addict. The truth is, forcing ourselves to go on as if nothing's happened, looks an awful lot like enabling.

Just Trust Me…

Martinkus addresses the faulty notion of 'if you'd forgiven me, you'd trust me', in *Worthy of Her Trust*.

'Forgiveness on its own is incredibly difficult for a person whose trust has been violated. When forgiveness becomes the focal point of trust building, the forgiver becomes the one

with the burden. The onus shifts off the violator and onto the forgiver. Realise that this backs the forgiver into a corner.[169]

Where Martinkus feels the true onus should lie will be discussed in the following chapter, on trust.

While the bible is clear that we need to forgive those who 'trespass against us', it does not tell us we need to trust the one forgiven: immediately, or ever. The only one the bible says we have to trust is God.

'Do not let your hearts be troubled. Trust in God; trust also in me.' John 14:1 (NIV)

My mother, the addictions counsellor, often reminds the partners of addicts that forgiveness is for the sake of the one forgiving – not for the sake of the perpetrator. Trust, is a completely separate issue from forgiveness and it is not recommended that wives try to marry the two. Trust should not happen until the addict has proven himself trustworthy.

From Grief to Forgiveness

After she got past her shock and denial, Shelley Martinkus says she began:

'...really just sitting in the pain and putting forgiveness to the side. I knew I needed to do it at some point, but I really tried not to put any pressure on myself to go there. I just felt like I had to sit in the pain and just ride it out.'[170]

Finally around twelve months after the first disclosure, she felt God begin to bring up the topic of forgiveness. She began to grapple with the concept. Soon after, she made a move in that direction.

Notice that for Shelley to get to the place where forgiveness was genuine and healing for both her and her husband, she had to grieve first. Grieving is the first step in the healing process. Without grieving, I'm not sure forgiveness is ever really possible. Why? Because if we've never accepted and processed what's been done to us, how do we forgive those things?

In *Beyond Boundaries*, Dr Townsend dedicates an entire chapter to 'grieving it and letting go.' In this chapter he warns,

'Without grief, the wound never becomes a memory. You remain stuck in re-experiencing the hurt and hard times over and over again. Much like someone who suffers from post-traumatic stress disorder, people who fail to grieve experience a cycle of repeated thoughts

and feelings, almost like flashbacks, that offer no relief. Grief ends this cycle and recalibrates your mind.[171]

For myself, I found that only after I had thoroughly grieved could I thoroughly forgive. However grieving was a process of many years for me. I'm not alone in that. What then, are the implications for forgiveness?

What Is Forgiveness?

In order to answer that question, we probably need to determine what exactly forgiveness is. Let's recap what I've presented about forgiveness so far. Forgiveness is not:

- Forgetting
- Trusting
- Repressing our emotions
- Going back to 'normal' ('normal' for him was acting out: you don't want 'normal')

That's a lot of… 'nots', but it doesn't really get us much closer to what forgiveness *is*.

There are entire books written on the subject of forgiveness, for the reason that it is somewhat mysterious and difficult to understand.

I'd like to begin our quest to grasp this concept by considering Richard Blankenship's definition of forgiveness: 'It is a long painful process that can bring healing'.[172]

Two words jump out at me here: 'process' and 'healing'.

Process

The word 'process' tells us forgiveness is not instantaneously achieved. There is obviously a single moment in time when we decide, 'yes, I will forgive', but that needs to work its way ever-deeper into our hearts. In the initial moment, I think what we are determining is that we want healing (for ourselves, and yes, even for the perpetrator) more than we want retribution. We're also determining we want God's will, whether or not it aligns with our feelings. As one pastor I know put it: 'forgiveness is being willing to take your hand off the throat of the one who wronged you.' I think that's a pretty good description of the initial decision to forgive.

However, since – like grieving – forgiveness is a process, we can expect that there will be growth into greater levels. Like the process of grieving, we want to invite God in to work with us. In fact, I suspect that some hurts cannot be forgiven without God's divine intervention. Understand that the moment we make a choice to forgive, God will meet us there and begin this work: until we grow into that place where we desire what is best for the one who has wronged us. That's a measure of more mature forgiveness.

In my experience, forgiveness is not a linear process. Sometimes, I get it. I'm there. I feel it. I can let go of the wrongs. Other times, I want retribution. Preferably with a blunt object and preferably in my hands. However, I find it helpful when I'm going down that track to consider:

- I don't have to feel 'forgiving' I just need to release my right for retribution to God
- Like M, I also deserve punishment for my sins – but God (the one I've hurt) chooses to forgive me
- Jesus is my model. His ability to forgive while in horrific pain, in fact while having the greatest injustice in the universe enacted on him, inspires me. It is one of the reasons He is my hero.

Finally, I try to remember that only God can take away this pain, put there by my husband. Retribution actually won't give me any relief (despite what Hollywood says).

....

> He blew up and we have had no contact since then (three years ago). I have forgiven him in my heart and feel compassion for him. I do not want or expect to see him again, and I hope that he has continued in his healing, is able to function more joyfully in life and has stopped hurting himself and others.
>
> — survey respondent

....

Healing

The other word that catches my attention in Blankenship's definition is the last one: 'healing'.

Like grieving, forgiveness is part of the healing process: for the victim and for others. While I stated earlier that forgiveness is not 'for the perpetrator', it can be an agent of healing in the relationship between victim and perpetrator. In fact, I believe forgiveness will always benefit the relationship to some degree: even if the relationship comes to an end.

Sound confusing? Consider that forgiveness has spiritual implications: for example, it's important for our own forgiveness (Matthew 6:14-15). Moreover, I believe that those spiritual implications don't apply only to individuals, but also to groups of people: thus forgiveness comes up in the (corporate) Lord's Prayer, and in Paul's exhortation to the Colossians about life in the body of Christ. (Colossians 3:13).

Forgiveness, then, is obviously a necessity if the marriage is to be healed. However, even if the marriage cannot be healed, our forgiveness will have positive effects on our ability to relate to our husband – and can be a powerful witness to an unrepentant man. Moreover, it will have positive effects on our children, on our extended family… possibly even on our broader communities.

Sound overly optimistic?

Strangely, God has used other aspects of my healing process to positively impact others. Remember the visualisation at the beginning of the chapter? Within a couple weeks of receiving that from the Lord, a sister – recently abandoned by her addict husband – mentioned she was 'dead, but still breathing.' This prompted me to relate my 'take a breath' story to her. I felt led to add that I had no idea where the 'cast-iron safe' in the visualisation came from. It certainly had nothing to do with my story.

She came back within a couple of hours to say she was in tears. Her husband had kept all his porn hidden in a cast-iron safe that he'd supposedly lost the combination to.

We both immediately understood that the visualisation of this intense grieving and pain was not just given to me… *for* me. It was given to me to help her with her pain. God was communicating his love and care to her while healing me.

The Process of Forgiveness

Harder (but not impossible) while we are in acute pain

Only slightly easier when there has been an apology

Easier when the apology was heartfelt (as opposed to fear or obligation-based)

Possible with God's assistance

Forgiveness and Love

A question I've asked myself along the way was, 'If I still feel angry and lash out, does it mean that I haven't forgiven?'

Like Shelley and Jason Martinkus, the answer I came up with was 'No.'

However, I realised those moment were a good time to take stock and review where I was in my forgiveness journey. If we're reliving anger, after our initial commitment to forgive, let's remind ourselves what the goal is (i.e., our freedom from pain, hatred and negative emotions). We can spend some time with God asking for his assistance in reaching this goal.

I've found that part of the process of forgiving M was learning to love him again. Like forgiveness, loving him was:

a. Not linear, and
b. Didn't involve my feelings for quite some time

Rather, it was simply a new mindset. It began with remembering that, 'this is God's son. He loves M. How does He want me to see him and behave toward him?'

> Most important of all, continue to show deep love for each other, for love covers a multitude of sins.
> —1 Peter 4:8 (NLT)

Jesus forgives us because he loves us.

Think back to the cross. Even though he was in immense pain, Jesus' love made him concerned for the retribution awaiting those persecuting him. Thus, he stated aloud to the Father that he wanted mercy rather than justice (i.e., retribution).

How do we model that? How do we love those who have despised us and the covenant they made with us? The answer: His help.

Our Abba enables us to survive, then grieve, then forgive… and love.

Taking it Further - Grieving

In order to forgive we need:

- Full disclosure (with the level of detail we want)
- A chance to accept and process the betrayal
- An opportunity to grieve that betrayal with God's support

Make a list of all the ways in which your husband's addiction has robbed you or changed your life for the worse. Consider as well its negative impact on your children and write their losses on your list.

Ask God to help you make this list. I've found that over the years, as He has changed my perspective… there have been more losses than I first realised – more depth to the betrayal than I initially saw. This has also meant more responsibility that I've had to bear for 'turning a blind eye' to dysfunction and allowing it to become the family norm.

Once your list is complete, ask God to sit with you and grieve each item. Afterward (and this process may take several days per item… don't rush it), I recommend you have a burial ceremony for it, or mark the passing of these various hopes and dreams in some other formal way. As you do, ask God to help you 'let go' of each wrong. Ask Him to restore what has been taken and fill you/your children with all the good things you needed from your husband, but didn't receive.

Understand this does not necessarily mark the end of your grieving. For myself it took four years before I was ready to grieve at a level that would help me to 'let go.' My mother (the addictions counsellor) says three to five years is a very common timeframe for the spouses of addicts to find deep healing from the pain the addiction has caused them.

For Reflection Ezekiel 37

Taking it Further – Forgiving

When it comes to forgiving there is more of our will involved than we might imagine. I had originally accepted that forgiveness would start with an act of will and that God would then have to take over from there.

Nevertheless, we must be an active participant for forgiveness to move forward. Have you made progress in the process of forgiving your husband? Do you understand that the forgiveness is more for you (your health) than for him?

If you have not started, or are stuck in your forgiveness journey spend some time journaling your thoughts on forgiveness. Ask yourself if there is something about forgiveness that frightens you.

Rather than journaling you can also write a poem or song, or draw/paint a picture that expresses your feelings on forgiveness and your forgiveness journey.

For Reflection: Colossians 3:12-17

Endnotes

166 Martinkus and Martinkus, 'Forgiveness' ibid.

167 Martinkus and Martinkus, ibid.

168 Blankenship, Spouses of Sex Addicts, p. 91.

169 Martinkus, *Worthy of Her Trust*, ebook, p. 113.

170 Martinkus and Martinkus, ibid.

171 J Townsend, *Beyond Boundaries: Learning to Trust Again in Relationships* (ebook), p. 134.

172 Blankenship, p. 58.

'Lucy, go back to bed.'

I point and my dog puts her tail between her legs and slinks back toward her bed beside the front door.

I close the lid to the chamber pot and pick my way through the dark room back to my own bed.

I've volunteered to do night duty in our half-finished house tonight. We have a rental in town as well – thanks to some friends who took pity on us. Still, we have animals that need tending to first thing in the morning and so we take turns spending our nights out at 'the land'.

In many ways our accommodation journey has mirrored our spiritual and emotional journeys. We've lived in rat-infested, uninsulated baches and leaky, mouldy caravans: all to get ourselves a little bit of land. Now we have the land, but our building process is hampered by lack of finances, grumpy neighbours, unscrupulous vendors and council. Greenhouse poly covers the windows and doors and our little place is freezing at night this time of year.

'Come dance with me, Lisa'

'Wh-what?'

'Come dance with me!'

'I'm not hearing you right, Lord. I could have sworn you asked me to come and *dance* with you... but it's the middle of the night, and it's freezing out there... and the dog will flip.'

'The dog will be fine.'

'I am *so* not hearing this right.'

I look out at the stars and the moon. It's such a beautiful night.

I'd fallen asleep peacefully a few hours ago, after a wonderful evening of praying and reading my bible. Could God actually be calling me to do something as crazy as dancing around the room with Him?

'Okay... I'll get out of bed and dance with you. But if the dog gets all worked up – and you know I just sent her back to bed and she's not far – then I'll know I'm imagining this... alright?'

I get out of bed and extend my arms as if around a waltz partner. I begin the steps... watching the door out of the corner of my eye.

Nothing. The dog is asleep and doesn't seem to notice me creaking across the floor. I smile and keep time to the random piece by Strauss playing in my head. 'Okay Jesus, this is fun... weird... but fun. Why are we doing this?'

'Will you let me love you?'

I freeze. 'What? Of course I want you to love me... that's all I've ever wanted is someone to love me... are you trying to say that *I'm* not letting you love me?'

Silence.

'This is nuts. How could you say that?' But my heart is sinking. Tears fill my eyes. I never would have come up with this one by myself, but He's right. I've got a lot of defences to keep people from hurting me. They're keeping love out too.

'Yes, Jesus. I'm so sorry I've been keeping your love out. Please change me. I want to know your love better.'

'Lisa: will you let me love you through M sometimes?'

I draw a sharp breath and plop down on my bed.

I stare out through the plastic window, eyes-narrowed. 'That's a good question. To be honest, Lord, I don't know if I'm ready for that yet.'

CHAPTER 16

Trust

I ended the last chapter saying that first God enables us to survive, then grieve, then forgive… then love. You'll notice that trust isn't in that list. The reason is that trust – at least in our spouse – is not necessary for our personal healing. It is only necessary for the healing of the relationship.

That said, if we have had our trust dealt a death blow by an unfaithful husband, it will take some healing in this area before we are able to trust others – particularly a man who may be interested in an intimate relationship with us. We may even need work in this area before we feel we can fully trust God.

Am I Ready to Trust?

In his indispensable book, *Beyond Boundaries: Learning to Trust Again in Relationships*, Dr Townsend devotes eight chapters to knowing when we are ready to trust others. In previous chapters, I have looked at what Townsend considers some of the necessary pre-requisites. These include taking stock of the damage, finding healthy support people to process with, setting healthy boundaries and grieving the hurt.

There are a few other ingredients necessary for trust that Dr Townsend explores in *Beyond Boundaries*. These include, understanding our own past choices, and connecting the dots.

These two concepts revolve around understanding how we got ourselves into a marriage with someone who was inclined to use us. If we haven't figured that out yet, we are far more likely to end up in another (or the same) relationship where we are deceived and betrayed.

Of course, any good therapist should be able to help us identify our relational patterns and their origin. Still, it doesn't hurt to do some of our own work here as well. Dr Townsend offers an exercise in *Beyond Boundaries* that anyone can do at home to help identify relational patterns and where in our past they came from. Townsend explains that this is an important process because,

'Unhealed relational wounds drive us to compulsive attempts to repair the damage. That is, without being aware of it, we seek out people we believe can "fix" what's wrong with us or help us find a piece of ourselves we feel is missing.'[173]

If we have unhealed emotional wounds, these often drive our desires. Once they are healed, our core values can take over and direct us to healthy relationships with people of solid character.

People are key to our healing and growth, so let's remember to ask God to lead us to the right ones. That means, the right therapists, prayer ministers, support groups and confidants. Let us also keep in mind that people alone aren't going to get us far. Healing and transformation are some of God's key works in our life (along with salvation). He is actively seeking to bring us to emotional and spiritual freedom and growth.

That growth, along with learning to hear Him more clearly, will help us know – 'Am I ready to trust?' and 'Do I trust this one?'

....

> I feel more trusting of him. I don't think I will ever 100% trust him completely as I once did. And I don't think I will ever feel toward him the way I once did. I am not the same woman as I was... [before] this happened.
>
> — survey respondent

....

Trusting 'him' Again

In *Beyond Boundaries*, Dr Townsend also teaches people to evaluate when another person is trustworthy. Evaluation is particularly important when we are thinking of removing some of our protective boundaries with someone who has wounded us. Explains Townsend,

'You need to see evidence of authentic transformation in order to move beyond boundaries with someone who has hurt you. That may seem like a difficult thing to assess, but there are at least four key pieces of evidence that characterise real heart change, all of which are observable – confession, ownership, remorse, and changed behaviour. The degree to which these things are evident – or absent – is the degree to which you can feel safe about trusting this individual again.'[174]

Let's take a closer look at these four key indicators of trustworthiness.

Confession and Ownership

Confession and ownership are two of the key ingredients of repentance. In a devotional I read recently I came across these thoughts on repentance:

'We repent when we name some act or attitude a sin. Then we admit our responsibility for that act or attitude. We acknowledge before God that "I am the one who did this, and I did it freely". Admitting our sin, we repudiate it and set ourselves to do things differently in the future. Note that repent is different from regret. Repenting is between me and God; regretting is mostly about me.'[175]

In Chapter 9, we looked at the issue of full disclosure. A man who is not willing to divulge his secrets and live in the light, is not even remotely worthy of trust. Moreover, if he is still playing the 'minimise, rationalise, justify and blame' game (see Chapter 6) – he is equally untrustworthy.

Perhaps our husband has confessed all (as far as we can ascertain) and owned it. There are, nevertheless, more subtle signs around confession to watch for. Is he becoming scrupulously honest? With himself? With others? As Jason Martkinus tells husbands, *"'I'd rather lose you than lie to you." As a person who betrayed your wife's trust, this must be your mantra.'*[176]

In Chapter 3 we looked briefly at Martinkus' advice to men with regards to a wife asking questions about the betrayal. His stand is that there needs to always be an open-door policy with regards to questions and processing of the disclosure. He tells men, who may be getting frustrated with repeating the story: *At that point, it's not about those details, it's about her husband receiving her heart right where she is.*[177]

Thus, if our husband is showing signs of impatience around our processing of his confession, we need to consider that he may not yet be very trustworthy.

> Remorse: it's not about you hating yourself more... but loving your victim more.

Remorse

Paul told the Corinthians, '…Your sorrow led you to repentance for you became sorrowful as God intended and so were not harmed in any way by us. Godly sorrow brings repentance that leads to salvation and leaves no regret, but worldly sorrow brings death.' –2 Corinthians 7:9-10 (NIV)

Godly sorrow, or remorse, is one of the most powerful agents of healing: for both perpetrator and victim. However, few people are able to readily distinguish between life-giving remorse and worldly sorrow (i.e., guilt). Dr Townsend puts it this way:

'Guilt without remorse simply punishes a person for his or her behaviour. There is no transformational experience in the relationship. The offender remains alone, beating himself up with his own club. That's why guilt never heals a character problem, a relationship, an addiction, or a soul…Remorse decreases the chances of the problem reoccurring. Guilt increases the likelihood of reoccurrence.'[178]

Our first good example of what true remorse may look like came from M's first counsellor, G. G's 'I get it' moment arrived four months into his recovery. That day, after God revealed to G the havoc he'd wreaked in his wife's life, he lay down on the floor and wept uncontrollably in God's presence for quite some time.

After relating this story to M, G said that it often takes a few months for a man to come to this point.

While the story was very helpful in explaining to M what remorse looks like, it was a bit of a stumbling block as well. Months went by, then years… no (or not many) tears came. There were many apologies, expressions of regret, but no display of serious heartfelt remorse.

So what was the problem? Ted Roberts sates in his book *Pure Desire*, 'A lack of remorse develops because they [sex addicts] go deep into dissociation. It is not that they don't care any more, but their shame level has reached staggering proportions. If they were totally and honestly to face what they are doing and what they have done to hurt others, they would go nuts.'[179]

It took over four years for M to have his 'I get it' moment. M's journey to reach this point included:

- Getting past 'hating himself more'
- Dealing with his emotional disconnectedness[180]
- Getting prayer ministry on multiple occasions
- Practicing Martinkus' amends matrix (see end of chapter)

Interestingly, after he had grieved thoroughly for what he'd done to me, M grieved for all the hurting women he'd used – as well as for how he'd hurt God with his actions. The dam had broken at last. Godly sorrow and healing were the result.

Restitution

Restitution is not included in Dr Townsend's list of observable signs; nevertheless, I believe it can be an important indicator of trustworthiness.

Admittedly, I never paid much attention to the details on restitution found in Exodus and Leviticus. To me, restitution seemed like an outdated concept in a day of Jesus' gift of salvation by grace. However, if I'd thought about it a little harder, I would not have been so quick to dismiss the ideas put forth in these books. Our God is never frivolous, and Jesus came to fulfil the law (Matthew 5:17-20).

However, it wasn't until I was doing some prayer ministry training, and the topic of restitution came up, that the light went on for me. In the training class, the teacher stated that the purpose of restitution was to restore trust.

Wow… of course. Restitution was about healing a broken relationship: not about punishing an offender. It suddenly made perfect sense.

But hold it. What could a man offer that would in any way make up for having devastated his wife's heart and life? There were only two things I could come up with: he could accept her boundaries, and support her in her quest for safety and healing.

Martinkus, in *Worthy of Her Trust*, comes to a similar conclusion. He examines restitution as a legal concept and then asks how men might apply it to their situation.

'What profit might we have gained that we could surrender to make our partner whole? The first thing is freedom. Violating trust through a breakdown of sexual integrity implies that you used your freedom to the detriment of your wife… In order to make things right and thus restore your wife to her previous state, you'll need to give up your freedom…I urge you to surrender the freedom to come and go as you please, the freedom to have

privacy, the freedom to talk to whomever you please, the freedom to be online at any time, the freedom to live without accountability, and the freedom to be lackadaisical in your relationship with your wife and with God.'[181]

He goes on to add that as part of restitution, a man also needs to give his wife freedom. This includes.

- *Freedom to ask any question at any time and for any reason*
- *Freedom to feel any emotion at any time and for any reason*
- *Freedom to be cynical, sceptical and incredulous*
- *Freedom to hold on to unforgiveness*

'Restitution requires you to give your wife permission to be authentic with her feelings rather than fearful of how you might respond, including your defensiveness.'[182]

Other ways he mentions to make restitution:

- Restore respect (including respecting her emotions)
- Offer your protection of her (and your children)
- Encourage – not just permit – the expression of her authentic feelings

Martinkus ends by saying that this kind of restitution makes amends as far as our cultural notion of the concept goes. Biblically – where the examples we are given involve giving back far more than was taken – it falls short. His 'amends matrix' (see end of chapter) brings men closer to a biblical notion of restitution and goes further in rebuilding trust.

....

> His lack of response or remorse has helped me to
> take the next step to move out of our relationship.
>
> — survey respondent

....

Changed Behaviour... and Character

M has changed enormously in the past four and a half years since we began this journey. Those changes occurred in this order: his intentions changed, then his actions, then his overall abilities and then his character. In other words he started with a change of will, then moved to a change of behaviour, which lead to changed habits. All these changes gradually percolated down into his heart, until his character was transformed.

Some men experience change in a different order. Sometimes it all begins with a miraculous transformation of character.

No matter the order of the steps, walking closer to God is key to any positive change. All the time M was growing, he was 'renewing his mind' by walking in closer communion with Father God than he had ever done before in his life.

Martinkus calls spiritual commitment one of the 'non-negotiables' of trust building.

'If your energy is directed at serving, loving, engaging the sanctification process, worshiping, and deepening your relationship with God, there is no space to act out sexually… [Your wife] knows the man God is calling you to be won't stomp on her heart. She can be confident the character he wants to develop in you will serve her with humility and love rather than serve yourself with arrogance and entitlement.'[183]

After a period of walking closer to God we can expect to see the development of the fruits of the Spirit. This can also be a good indicator that he is becoming trustworthy.

To evaluate this factor, we can ask ourselves where our husband was weak in the past. Obviously self-control, for one. Do we see improvement here? Let's look at our husbands' other addictions or habitual indulgences that don't lead toward sanctification… have there been any changes? What about patience? Most addicts are highly short on this fruit. And as Steve Arterburn states in *Every Heart Restored*,

'His patience is a sign of deep repentance. If that sign isn't there, it's a troubling red flag. When your husband demands immediate forgiveness and doesn't show patience, that's an indication that he's not where he needs to be.'[184]

Another sign of genuine remorse, that flows out of spiritual growth, is a willingness to do anything to get healthy. When our husbands genuinely reach this point, they don't rely on us to keep them in line. Instead, they show an eagerness to implement whatever healthy habits are needed to ensure recovery: installing internet filters, placing the computer in an open area in the home, swapping the 'smart' phone for a dumb phone, etc.

Obviously such behaviours can be adopted by our husbands out of a sense of fear, rather than because they deeply desire to be transformed. Character changes can be 'faked' for a while… but not forever. We need to be on the look out for consistent change over a long period of time. As Dr Townsend says,

'If you have experienced tough times with a person, you want the problem behaviour to

change over time – we hope forever. Pretty much anyone can change a behaviour in the short term. It's called being on good behaviour, and we all learned that at school – get the behaviour under control and get out of trouble. But if you're going to make yourself vulnerable to someone, you need to know that the change will be sustained for days, which lead to weeks, months, and years. Then you can gradually trust again.[185]

> I am still struggling because no one believes my husband could do these things as he appears to be soft, gentle, kind and spiritual, but he is far from these things. I need real help!! — survey respondent

Trusting a Spiritualiser

Now, some husbands were uber-religious to begin with and may have used spiritualising as a means to control and abuse their wives. How does an interest in God and things spiritual prove that he's changing when this is the case?

Martinkus talks about the fact that the hyper-religious betrayer exhibits certain unhealthy behaviours. These include confessions with minimising (e.g., 'I'm struggling with temptation' as opposed to 'I'm a serial adulterer'), and using scripture to advance a selfish agenda (e.g., you're not to withhold yourself from me – so start enabling my addiction by being my personal prostitute). This is, of course, a form of spiritualising. I've also seen people centre the abuse around spiritual giftings (you just don't have the same prophetic giftings I do) and other spiritual theories that have some biblical basis (e.g., your judgements against your parents in childhood are to blame for my addiction).

Another common 'dodge', as he calls it, is for the religious husband to say that his wife needs to leave the judging to the Holy Spirit. To such a man Martinkus says, 'Dude, give me a break! That's just a chintzy way of saying, "Stop demanding that I step up and be the kind of man and husband you deserve."'[186]

If that is what we have been faced with in the past, obviously a key change we are looking for is our husband's willingness to apply the Word to himself (even when it hurts) rather than simply to other people – when it's to his benefit. He will need to focus on how his own sin is at the root of his problems, and not blame our sins.

Moreover, such a man usually lacks an understanding of God's grace and love: balanced with His truth and justice. When he begins to let go of religion and to embrace a relationship with God – the eternal source of life, love and goodness – he's taken a necessary step toward re-establishing his credibility as a husband.

> I don't know for sure if I can trust him. But he's been taking more ownership of how his actions have hurt me and our marriage. — survey respondent

Amends Matrix

M has been given many exercises to do in recovery. None has been as effective in healing both him and our relationship as Jason Martinkus' 'amends matrix' as described in *Worthy of Her Trust*.

The amends matrix is a seven-step process, to be initiated by the husband, wherein he identifies his wife's present pain, owns the part his past betrayal plays in that pain, empathises with her and then casts a vision for her healing in the future.

It sounds simple – and in many ways it is – but for most men it requires a bit of practice. Done even slightly wrong, the amends matrix can add to a woman's hurt. Done well, it can enable a man like M to feel his wife's pain and grieve it before her in a way that is incredibly healing.

However, I'm not sure that the amends matrix would have been as effective earlier in our healing journey. A man who has fundamental character issues (e.g., with honesty, patience, selfishness, fearfulness) has to show consistent change in these areas before a breakthrough in an area such as empathy is likely to occur. And even if it should occur before growth in these other areas: it is only one piece of the 'you can trust me now' puzzle.

Trusting Others

For many (statistically speaking, over half of us), reading this last section will have been painful. We have not had this type of validation of our suffering from the one who betrayed us (I'm thinking of my first marriage now), and it's likely that we never will. Our relationship is over, or on its deathbed.

Understand that our ability to trust has been materially damaged by this experience. However, we don't have to live behind a stone wall for the rest of our life for fear of being devastated again. As Dr Townsend says, 'we need to move beyond our self-protection because we are inevitably and permanently drawn to connect with others.'[187]

This desire is God-given. It draws us to Him, as well as into community. When we shield ourselves from harm, we also end up keeping out those who would help us heal and enjoy life again.

Isolating is tempting – I know. However, we truly can learn from the mistakes of the past and live to have better relationships. We can ask God to teach us and lead the way toward healthier people. Let's start with those who love us and then consider professionals and those who share our experience of betrayal, but who are healing.

Of course, we may have trouble trusting God right now. If that's the case, we can tell him so. God's big enough to take it, and it's not the first time he's heard it either. More than anything else, he wants to keep the dialogue going. As part of that, we should keep reading his love letter to us (the bible) so that he has a chance to respond. Let's listen for His still, small voice, look in nature and in others for reflections of His love and tenderness toward us. Let's take the time to grieve our pain with Him.

Once we learn again that we can trust our perfect creator, we can move on to trusting his less than perfect creation.

Taking it Further

There's a saying in recovery circles: believe actions, not words. Do your husband's actions say he is trustworthy? Even if his actions seem like the right ones, have they been right over a long period of time?

Some addicts are very co-dependent and offer improved behaviour in order to control their wives, or with the expectation of something in return. Ask God to help you discern if this is the case with your husband. Generally speaking: time will tell if he is undergoing a fundamental transformation, or a guilt and fear-based change of behaviour at the surface level.

One of the advantages of watching for sustained, consistent change, is that it requires time. Many addicts need time to leave behind their selfish ways and experience transformation in God. For most, it is not an overnight process.

However, trust isn't a light switch that can only be 'on' or 'off'. We can gradually trust more as we determine that our husbands are becoming more trustworthy.

Make a list of areas you in which you would want to see you husband grow before you would consider trusting him more.

Are there areas (in yourself) you would need healed before you could trust more? Are these areas affecting your ability to trust anyone besides your husband?

For Reflection: Isaiah 42:3

Endnotes

173 Townsend, ibid, p. 122.

174 Townsend, ibid, p. 345.

175 J Tetllow, *Face What's Wrong by Praying the Examen*, <http://bit.ly/1wlLiko>.

176 J Martinkus, *Worthy of her Trust*, p. 145.

177 Martinkus and Martinkus, 'Talking it Through', ibid.

178 Townsend, ibid, p. 354.

179 T Roberts, *Pure Desire*, p. 70.

180 Much direction for this was gleaned from Dr Townsend's book: *Loving People: How to Love and Be Loved*.

181 Martinkus, ibid, p. 260-261.

182 Martinkus, ibid, p. 261.

183 Martinkus, ibid, p. 134-135.

184 S Arterburn, F Stoeker, B Stoeker, M Yorkey, *Every Heart Restored: A Wife's Guide to Healing in the Wake of a Husband's Sexual Sin*, Double Day Religious Publishing Group, 2009.

185 Townsend, ibid, p. 359.

186 Martinkus, ibid, p. 138.

187 Townsend, ibid, p. 27.

I search Ms eyes. It's strange: I see only love, joy, and peace.

I have known him 14 years, and this is the first time I have not caught a shadow of fear, avarice or something sinister in those eyes... even while we were in each others arms.

'I can see so deeply into you right now. You're becoming a good man.'

The eyes film over. 'There's still some bad stuff in there, I can feel it. But you're right. Something is changing.'

The tears fall and he holds me tighter.

CHAPTER 17

Intimacy

Whether we recognise it or not, most of us spend an enormous amount of our lives searching for intimacy. Our thoughts, our choices, our actions all propel us in the direction we hope to find it.

Why?

Because we were created to live in union. Adam and Eve walked with God in the garden. Theirs was a holy, fulfilling, three-in-one relationship. Humans are created in the image of a three-in-one God.

Then sin came. It destroyed the union, it destroyed our ability to be 'naked and not ashamed.' What it didn't destroy was the longing to get back to that communion with God and man, or God's determination to make that possible again.

Thus, Jesus chose to comfort the apostles before his death by telling them: 'On that day you will realise that I am in my Father, and you are in me, and I am in you.' (John 14:20 NIV).

One of Satan's greatest lies is that intimacy equals sex. Another is that intimacy equals romance. The truth is that intimacy is a heart and mind connection with God and others – a deep 'knowing'.

In his extremely important work, *Wired for Intimacy: How Pornography Hijacks the Male Brain*, Dr William Struthers explains the desire for intimacy this way:

'Relational drives (including the sexual drive) propel us toward each other and toward God.

In connecting with each other and knowing one another, we sample the transcendence of God… Whether that transcendence is found in sexual union with a spouse or in the selfless giving of our time and affection to others, we can discover something outside of ourselves and experience the love, holiness and goodness of the Creator as we give selflessly to others.[188]

Intimacy is what we were created for.

Intimacy	communion with God and others
	being profoundly known
It's About:	transcending our finitude
	the giving of ourselves

Intimacy: The Answer to Addiction and More

True, transcendent intimacy helps cure the desire for frivolous encounters – such as sex addicts regularly seek out. Says Struthers:

'When the need to be known is met regularly, the sexual drive is decreased. When it is not regularly satisfied, the force of it builds. As the drive increases, we become less able to make wise decisions about how we meet it. A starving man will eat anything that is put before him. An intimacy-neglected man will grasp at any available opportunity to know or be known. The need for intimacy will build without emotional connection, and he will look for this connection in unhealthy and unproductive places (such as pornography, strip clubs or prostitutes). These places and experiences do not truly meet the need for intimacy, so the drive will return quickly. It is only temporarily assuaged by these imposters. These emotional experiences are designed to have relational objects – real people – which anchor them.[189]

And in that intimate knowing with real people, we not only connect with God, but our deepest longings are met. In *Surfing for God*, pastor and counsellor Michael J Cusick describes seven great human longings.

- Attention – I long for people to like me. I long for your embrace.
- Affection – I long to be enjoyed. I long to be delighted in. I long for you to take pleasure in who I am.
- Affirmation – I long to know I have what it takes. I long for your blessing.

- Acceptance – I long to belong. I long to be desired.
- Satisfaction – I long for fullness. I long for well-being.
- Significance – I long for impact. I long for meaning. I long to be powerful.
- Security – I long to know I will be okay.[190]

Sex and romance purport to meet our longings. However, these are only the scraps under the table: not the feast God has in mind for us. The prostitute does not actually delight in her john. Our Casanova may appear to take pleasure in 'who we are', but he may only be taking pleasure in the shape of our buttocks.

Moving from these frivolous encounters, though to true intimacy, requires health. It also requires that we get past the common barriers to intimacy.

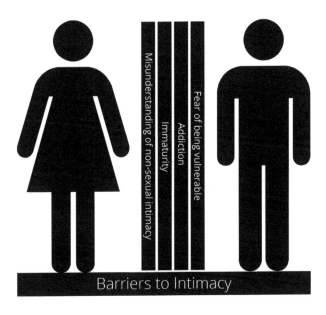

Barriers to Intimacy

Fear of Being Vulnerable

Jason Martinkus describes intimacy as, 'A state of honesty, openness, vulnerability, transparency and authenticity with oneself, God and/or another person.'[191]

One of the reasons the lies of 'intimacy equals sex' and 'intimacy equals romance' are so compelling is that the idea of being 'honest, open, vulnerable, transparent and authentic' is terrifying to most people. We've been hurt. We've done shameful things we want to hide. We'll be rejected if we are fully known.

Fear of vulnerability is one of the key ingredients in many men's sexual addictions. Sex is offered free and easy all around them: no messy emotions, no exposing themselves with a chance of rejection. TV, movies, videogames all tell men to flee the vulnerability necessary for meaningful relationships, and instead seek out power over others.

With sex we get the ecstatic high (followed by peace) without the need to be vulnerable. Romance gives us something similar. Why bother with the intimacy stuff then?

Remember Dr Townsend's quote on great relationships involving risk? (See Chapter 13). That's why. Vulnerability offers the greatest pay-offs.

But perhaps vulnerability is a new concept for us, where do we begin?

Jesus.

Jesus is our model for vulnerability. None of us will ever be asked to lay down power such as He had and put ourselves so completely into the hands of those who desire to destroy us. He did that so we could be one with Him and the Father. If we ask, He will help us move forward into the vulnerability necessary to enjoy that union.

Moreover, as we ourselves become more mature and healthy, we will attract people with whom it is safe to be vulnerable. Our sensors that detect those kinds of people will become more fine turned. Vulnerability should always be reserved for the right people. If our husband has not yet proved himself trustworthy, then we need to exercise wisdom about how vulnerable we make ourself to him.

Addiction

Struthers argues that while godly sexuality drives us toward intimacy, unhealthy sexuality drives us toward compulsions – aka, addiction.

'With each lingering stare, pornography deepens a Grand Canyon-like gorge in the brain through which images of women are destined to flow… They [addicts] have unknowingly created a neurological circuit that imprisons their ability to see women rightly as created in God's image. Repeated exposure to pornography creates a one-way neurological superhighway where a man's mental life is over-sexualized and narrowed… The mental life is fixated on sex, but it is intended for intimacy.'[192]

Once a sexual addiction, or 'superhighway' has come into the picture, sex, instead of propelling us towards others, drives us inward. Moving towards others, then, becomes a painful reminder of our shameful behaviour. I believe this pain is the reason so many sex addicts lash out against those around them in anger and violence.

Of course sexual addiction isn't the only addiction that creates a barrier to intimacy. Any addiction puts up a wall between us and God or others. Interestingly 'anything that creates a barrier between us and God' is also a definition of sin. Sin is, of course, the mother of all intimacy killers.

Australian Christian sexologist, Dr Patricia Weerakoon puts it this way:

'Part of the craziness, irrationality and un-healthiness of sin is that it makes us insensitive to the greatest lover in the universe (God in Christ), and to the greatest act of love in history (Jesus' death and resurrection), and makes us go running after other lovers instead (other religions, money, wealth, prosperity, romance, etc.). None of these can ultimately satisfy.[193]

The good news is, there is hope for addicts. Just as unhealthy neurological pathways were formed by repetitive behaviour, so new neurological pathways can be formed by repetitive right thinking and behaviour. We can indeed be transformed by the renewing of our mind! (Romans 12:2) According to Struthers, men need to fight addiction with addiction:

The process of sanctification is an addiction to holiness, a compulsive fixation on Christ and an impulsive pattern of compassion, virtue and love. This is what we are wired for. This is what we are meant for.[194]

Immaturity

Not only do we need emotional and spiritual health to experience intimacy, we need maturity. This is another character trait that is commonly misunderstood.

Women, for example, often assume that a man who is interested in religious or spiritual matters is mature. While spiritual maturity is a good start toward emotional maturity, the latter does not necessarily follow the former. Moreover, as already mentioned, many a sex addict is attracted to hyper-religious behaviour. There can be an enormous difference (think the apostles vs the pharisees) between a man engaging God and sanctification, and a man into rules and religion.

Moreover, women also frequently assume that a man who is a strong communicator – who knows how to set a romantic scene and tell her what she likes to hear – is mature. As Dr Townsend explains,

'Love is not enough. Nor are attentiveness, romantic feelings, a charming personality, great competencies and skills, or promises to change. You need substance underneath the topping. Don't sell yourself short. Character always wins over time.'

Maturing is a life-long process: so long as we don't get stuck. Trauma, neglect, and our own sin can de-rail our maturation process. Finding healing for our wounds and forgiveness for our sins (as well as forgiving others) are the first steps in maturing. The therapists at Shepherd's House also talk about the need for life-giving relationships.[195]

There is no definitive list of maturity traits. However, I believe the list below, synthesised from multiple sources, gives us a good starting point for evaluating our own and others' maturity. The mature individual has:

- The desire and capacity to love
- The capacity to live in joy and peace
- The ability to trust
- The ability to set healthy boundaries
- The ability to receive and give
- The ability to persist and persevere
- The ability to take responsibility for her own actions
- The desire and ability to care for others in his family and beyond
- The ability to be vulnerable and authentic
- The desire and ability to serve and protect others
- The ability to give without expecting in return
- The ability to be the same person in all circumstances
- The ability to accept others where they are at and value them
- The ability to support others who are experiencing difficult emotions

If that list seems a bit depressing, take heart. We need to be on the road to developing these abilities: we don't have to master them by the end of the week. Jesus – the only one I know who has all these traits perfected – wants to lead our journey to maturity: to 'Christ-likeness.'

Moreover, we can't expect to find all these traits in those with whom we hope to have intimate relationships. As Dr Townsend says, 'Certainly no one is perfect, and finding a perfect person is not the goal. But perfect is a long way from dark.'[196]

> Therefore confess your sins to each other and pray for each other so that you may be healed. —James 5:16

Misunderstanding of Non-Sexual Intimacy

When I speak to teenaged girls on the topic of intimacy, I ask if they think that intimacy is only about sex. So far, I've only ever heard, 'No, of course not!' Girls and women intuitively understand that there are many opportunities for intimate relationships in this life: parent-child, friend-friend, God-child. Any relationship where we can trust, be vulnerable, give of our heart and receive another's.

For men, however, non-sexual intimacy is not well understood. Says Struthers:

The myths of masculinity in our culture have isolated men from each other and impaired their ability to honour and bless one another. Too many men have too few intimate male friends. Their friendships run only as deep as the things they do together.[197]

Perhaps it's not surprising that when an addict comes out and confesses, one of the first thing he looks for are other men, to connect with, who share his struggle. Jason Martinkus devotes an entire chapter of *Worthy of Her Trust* to showing men how to find honourable accountability partners with whom to walk through recovery. The purpose of accountability partners, he argues, is not only to restore a wife's trust, but also to find healing.

Of course, it's possible to have shallow accountability relationships. It's also possible to fake recovery. Deep healing is found in deep relationships. Says Martinkus, 'It [accountability] is about digging into the nitty-gritty of each other's lives and being known.'[198]

He recommends that men meet weekly to pray and talk. The discussion should include an update on sexual integrity, feelings experienced, one's spiritual journey, the journey toward marital restoration, and something each man is committed to do in the next week to grow.

Having these kinds of friendships – where we are fully known and still accepted by our peers – is really a pre-requisite to marital intimacy. Moreover, as men and women create intimate bonds with other believers, we create what Martinkus calls, 'a legacy of connection' for our children. Such a legacy has the potential to positively impact the communities of the future.

> I wasn't willing to be intimate with someone I don't feel safe with. — survey respondent

Non-Sexual Intimacy in Marriage

Men don't just struggle with bringing non-sexual intimacy into their friendships. They struggle with bringing it into their marriage as well.

When a man and woman tackle his betrayal – and her trauma – as a team, they will find many opportunities to grow in the area of non-sexual intimacy. Last chapter I talked about Martinkus' amends matrix. Exercises like this provide a perfect opportunity to discuss the difficult things of the heart together. As couples share together, cry together, and pray together, they are forging a path into a deeper, more meaningful relationship. Our intimacy is maturing.

I love what Struthers says about non-sexual, maturing intimacy between a husband and wife:

'Maturing intimacy is more than a romantic attraction or sexual chemistry. It is rooted in the agape love that we are to have for one another. It is marked by forgiveness, mercy, grace and perseverance. We have the emotional and spiritual drives to develop a relationship which meets our needs to know and to be known by another, but these needs find their fulfilment when they align with God's direction as revealed in Scripture. When those drives are properly directed, the result is truly beautiful to behold: a husband and wife who have devoted themselves to each other.'[199]

As already mentioned in previous chapters, many wives need a period of abstinence following disclosure. This is a perfect time for the husband who is dedicated to healing the relationship to begin growing his non-sexual intimacy with his wife.

For some women, intimate conversation, or physical contact, have always been a prelude to sex. If this was the case for you, it will be hard to take your husband's initial overtures of intimacy at face value. If, like mine, your husband is intimacy averse, you may find that he's suspicious of *your* overtures of intimacy. Whichever role we find ourselves in, we should try to be patient and persist in showing him that a couple can in fact, connect lovingly: no strings attached.

Some women have stated that their husbands find touching them – without advancing to sex – impossible. Some women struggle with the same issue. In such cases, today is the day for the struggling party to ask God to develop in them the fruit of self-control. Of course, if you both want things to escalate to sex, that's fine too. However, remember that learning to engage in non-sexual intimacy will have many benefits for your relationship. This includes benefits in the bedroom at another point.

As Dr Townsend says:

'The order of matters is this: listen and talk at a deeper level first, and put sex second. Especially for women, who are often relationally ahead of men, being heard and understood makes women feel loved and safe and opens the door to their own passion and desire. In this way, both the husband and the wife learn how to connect with each other, learn how to put the other person first, learn to value patience and relationship, and then experience sexuality as a result… make sure that, in the main, emotional intimacy trumps sexual intimacy.'

The most amazing purpose of marital sex is evangelism. Mutually caring, fulfilling, life-bringing sex between a man and a woman who have committed themselves to each other for life, points to the teachings of Jesus Christ… The virtues that characterise the gospel – other-focused care, commitment and sacrifice – demonstrate both the character of the Triune God himself, and the character of good sex in a healthy marriage.

— Dr Patricia Weerakoon

Sexual Intimacy

For many of us, sex has become tainted. We relate it now to pain, betrayal, rejection: even spiritual defilement. But that's not what God had in mind for us when he gave us the excellent gift of our sexuality.

In *Sexuality and Holy Longing*, Lisa McMinn describes sexuality as:

'A fundamental part of what it means to be human. How we understand it and experience it is integral as we discover who we are and it points us to our Creator. While it is

fundamental to our being, our sexuality is not about sexual intercourse. Our sexuality is one of the sources of the restlessness in our lives. It drives us to search for intimacy where we can be fully known and where we can know another. It is in this place of intimacy where the experience of the ecstatic is sometimes met and we are able to transcend our physical limitations and understand in part the transcendent nature of God.[200]

Our sexual longings drive us toward intimacy with another human being. They offer a taste of the ecstasy that is found when we are in communion with God.

Sounds good in theory. However, it may seem a far cry from the sexual relationship we are currently experiencing with our betrayer husband. Until a man gets healing for his addiction, and begins to rebuild intimacy with his wife, he is likely to experience some of the following during sex:

- Flashbacks to the porn/other partners
- Difficulty becoming aroused by us
- Loss of erection related to flashbacks and shame
- A tendency to objectify and focus on our parts
- Premature or delayed ejaculation

Moreover, our husband may try and use sex as a means of manipulating us or feeding his addiction (see Chapter 10).

Likewise many women find it impossible not to wonder obsessively who/what he is really thinking about, who else he's done this with, what kind of diseases he might be carrying…[201] all manner of triggering thoughts.

All in all, it seems a recipe for disaster.

It is impossible to stress enough how important it is for a betrayed wife to consider if she and her husband are truly ready to re-enter the arena of sexual intimacy. As Patricia Weerakoon says: 'The relationship of sex is the most intimate of the earthly relationships. Sexual arousal and orgasm cements a body, soul and spirit bond between partners.'[202]

Hopefully you have read the previous chapter on Trust (Chapter 16). From the information there you've probably realised that if you do not trust someone you don't want to be cementing your body, soul and spirit to him.

However, assuming your relationship is healthy enough to move forward into sexual intimacy, there are things you can do to feel safer and begin to grow in this area:

- Pray: as weird as it may sound, invite God into your sexual relationship. Ask him to make it about intimacy and love.
- Talk and connect: as mentioned in the previous section, connect without sex first. Also, agree to keep the sexual pressure off. Your intimacy doesn't *have* to become sexual. Relax and see where it goes.
- Keep lights on and eyes open: seeing you will help your husband reprogramme his brain with regards to what is perceived as sexually exciting. Seeing your eyes and face will help him to follow your emotions and stay emotionally connected.
- Keep talking: practice expressing how you feel about what he's doing, and what you are thinking. Encourage him to do the same.
- Stop before intercourse.

What was that?

While not necessary, I recommend the programme outlined in *The Best Sex for Life*, by Christian sexologist Patricia Weerakoon. Dr Weerakoon believes that bonding/healing takes place better when couples ease their way toward intercourse over a number of weeks. In the interim, they practice physical intimacy that does not involve intercourse.[203]

Because she is not writing specifically for those with sexual addiction, not all of Weerakoon's advice (e.g., around sex toys) should be adopted by couples where there has been betrayal/addiction. Refer back to Martinkus' advice around porn-star-experience sex (Chapter 10). Nevertheless, the overall gist of the programme – when preceded by other work in the areas of recovery, growth and emotional intimacy – may prove helpful to couples moving back into sexual intimacy.

Above all, let's make intimacy the focus of our sexual expression. Intimacy is not just knowing the other's body, it's about knowing each other's hearts. If despite this re-focusing, we are still struggling with pervasive, negative thoughts, we should step back. Instead, we can practice intimacy with God and others (see next section), then non-sexual intimacy with our husband again.

If your husband is really where he needs to be to engage in intimacy with you: he will wait out your healing. If he is pressing you on this, it's a sign he may not be ready. Explain to him why you need to proceed slowly. Let him know that experts feel that intimacy (as opposed to sex) is healing for him too. See if he rises to the challenge.

If he does, you'll probably find, as I did, that intimacy is a healing balm to a weary heart. It strengthens the relationship as nothing else. It draws us to each other and into the heart of God in unfathomable ways.

Intimacy for Singles

Sadly, sexual intimacy is a thing of the past for many betrayed wives – if it was ever part of the picture.

If this is your case, I encourage you to grieve your loss in this area. It is a tragedy to come to the threshold of sexual intimacy and be denied entrance. Know that this will not always be the case. Jesus has gone to prepare a place for you: that where He is, you may be also (John 14:3).

Some days that may seem like small comfort. It's okay to tell God that. Ask him to draw you even now into His heart. As part of this, you may want to spend some time meditating on oneness with Jesus and the Father. Pour out your heart to Him and ask Him questions of an intimate nature. 'What do you see as special about me? Why do you love me? How do you see me?' Let Him speak goodness into your soul.

Ask Him, as well, to send you others with whom you can enjoy non-sexual intimacy. As you heal from betrayal, and grow in God, you will be better able to enjoy rich, life-giving relationships. You will be ready to enter into true communion. As Drs Judy and Jack Balswick say,

'Communion with God and one another is the answer to the longing that our very nature craves. It can be found in friendships, the body of Christ, the expression of our sexuality and in many other ways. The mercy, grace and healing that can be found along the way both deepens our need for communion and our ability to have it.'[204]

Taking it Further

Our relationship with our husband will never be what it once was (if we felt we were his first love, or primary love). However, if we are still together, there remains a possibility of re-attaching, exploring intimacy together, and moving on to a deeper more mature relationship.

For those who are married:

Do you think it's possible to practice a degree of detachment while also exploring intimacy with your husband?

What do you see as holding your husband back from greater levels of intimacy? Have you shared that with him?

Have you ever had your husband 'fall' in his addiction (lusting, porn, etc.) shortly after you were intimate with him? How did you deal with the pain? How long did it take to heal from the incident? Have you learned any techniques (journaling, praying, talking to others, removing yourself physically from his presence) that help reduce the time of healing? Does it help you to visualise God as the end receiver of the gift of yourself?

For Reflection: The Song of Solomon.

For all women:

What do you see as the current obstacles to your ability to experience intimacy at present? What might be a 'next step' in getting past that obstacle?

For Reflection: John 14

Endnotes

188 Struthers, ibid, ebook p. 288.

189 Struthers, ibid, p. 294.

190 MJ Cusick, *Surfing for God: Discovering the Divine Desire Beneath Sexual Struggle*, Thomas Nelson, 2012, ebook p. 83.

191 Martinkus, ibid, p. 100.

192 Struthers, ibid. p. 152.

193 P Weerakoon, retrieved August 2014, <http://patriciaweerakoon.com/sexual-integrity-in-a-sexualised-world/>.

194 Struthers, ibid, print book, p. 263.

195 Wilder et al., ibid, p. 35.

196 Townsend, ibid, p. 108.

197 Struthers, ibid, p. 257.

198 Martinkus, ibid, p. 215.

199 Struthers, ibid, p. 302.

200 L McMinn, *Sexuality and Holy Longing: Embracing Intimacy in a Broken World*, Wiley, 2004.

201 As already mentioned, no woman should entertain having intercourse with a newly discovered sex addict until both she and he have been tested for STIs.

202 P Weerakoon, 'Porn: the Ultimate Idolatry', May 18, 2013, retrieved August 2013, <http://patriciaweerakoon.com/porn-the-ultimate-idolatry/>.

203 This technique, known as sexual reintegration, is also outlined in *A Couple's Guide to Intimacy* by Dr Bill Bercaw.

204 J Balswick and JO Balswick. *Authentic Human Sexuality: An integrated Christian Approach*, InterVarsity Press, 1999.

Across the hall I see a line up of teenage boys. They are standing in front of my husband, waiting to talk to him.

It's been an insane couple of days. We were up until 1:00 am last night trying to finish off our presentations: all four. Between the two of us, we've given six presentations to youth leaders today: one each on media literacy, two each on sex vs intimacy.

Because we were presenting simultaneously I never got to sit in on one of M's sessions. I have no idea yet, how they went. He was a bit of a wreck last night with anticipation nerves.

I was sad to see that while his media literacy session was packed, only a few of the young men were willing to attend his first presentation on sexuality this morning: a talk that was repeated this afternoon.

I, on the other hand, had a solid group of girls for both my morning talks.

Fortunately, before our repeat performance this afternoon, a doctor – well known to the group – introduced our presentations saying, 'This isn't your usual "don't do it" church-talk on sex, guys. This presentation is packed full of the latest research on all the issues. Get in there.'

A flood of boys then poured into M's presentation room, and the doors closed.

I smile again at the memory of it as I pack up my laptop.

The line of young people is getting smaller now so I approach M and our son who is standing beside him, beaming. I arrive as an enormous teenager – a boy who is from the roughest neighbourhood in our city – grabs M by both shoulders and presses his nose against his, in a traditional Maori *hongi*. 'Thank you, man,' the teen whispers.

M turns to me and our eyes meet. I see the tears threatening to spill over. My bottom lip begins to tremble.

This is redemption.

CHAPTER 18

Juggernaut

When I think about the pornography industry, trafficking industry, and the entertainment industry I often visualise a large steamroller. Not just large… but supernaturally enormous. That steamroller hasn't just flattened me, and you, and our families. It's flattening entire nations. Like ours.

I find it exceedingly painful to watch Christians adopt the 'don't talk about it,' mantra when it comes to sex. As Gordon Dalbey says: 'That's sad. Worse, it's dangerous. Banning sexuality from church leaves a vacuum which the world is literally hell-bent to fill.'[205]

Some Christians make an exception on this ban for such issues as homosexual marriage, and abortion: symptoms of the greater problem.

And while we denounce these seemingly remote ills (though in reality they're at our church doorsteps), most of us are actually supporting the sexual brokenness and dysfunction at the root of these issues by our lifestyle choices and inaction.

Below are some of the truths M and I talk about with young people… in the hope that they will join us in becoming agents of change.

The Truth About Media

Sexualised portrayals of women on billboards, mainstream print media, prime-time television and even family-rated movies are setting men and boys up for sexual addiction.

Videogames are infamous for their sexualised depictions of females and for rewarding men for engaging in the behaviours of sexual addiction[206] and misogyny. However, from the news to sports events, Christian dramas to sit-coms: women are increasingly portrayed as valuable only for their beauty and sex appeal.

The definition of 'beauty' we see portrayed in media is exceedingly narrow. The pinnacle of media beauty is achievable only by a small percentage of teens and young women: and then only with the help of others including make-up artists, hairstylists, post-production artists and, increasingly, surgeons.

Thus our young women are becoming ill chasing after an impossible goal. Literally ill, as they diet, dye-it and buy-it trying to meet some impossible goal for their height, weight, skin clarity, breast size, butt shape and wardrobe. Psychologically they are becoming damaged by the constant message that their main purpose in life is to please men sexually and that if they fail in the 'hot' department, they haven't got a chance.

Boys are getting this same message: that girls' only value is in their looks and that relationships with them are primarily about sexual stimulation. Studies show:

- Overexposure to erotic stimuli (such as those in media) exhaust the sexual responses of normal, healthy young men.[207]
- Media creates an obsession with *looking at* women rather than interacting with them. It feeds male obsession with visual stimulations and trivialises other mature features of a healthy sexual relationship.
- Media creates an attitude in which women are objects rated by size, shape and harmony of body parts. Sexual fantasy leads to emotional unavailability and dissatisfaction (with 'average' women or familiar ones).[208]

As men increasingly use pornography they become increasingly impotent. You see, that's part of the pornographic experience; you become impotent in the sense that you cannot function without having images... Impotent means 'without power', and the male is indeed without his own power after becoming addicted to pornography; he has to rely on the power that's given to him by one of these pictures or films.

— Dr Judith Reisman

The Truth About the Blurring Line between Media and Porn

If media gets them started, porn solidifies boys' and men's sexual addictions.

However there's no longer a hard distinction between 'media' (e.g., television, movies, games) and porn. Struthers says, 'many things on television or on newsstands [are] pornographic… Pornography… is everywhere. You cannot get away from it; if you don't view it intentionally, you will unintentionally.'[209]

Other researchers agree: today's media is the soft-core porn of ten years ago. The actual 'pornography industry' has gone entirely hardcore now.[210]

And if you're thinking, 'well that soft-core stuff isn't really so bad,' Struthers states that soft porn is more damaging to the brain than hardcore.[211]

Entertainment producers, when pressured to behave more ethically, often try to hide behind the 'but it's art' excuse. A recent online blog post by videographer, Cap Stewart, details stories about mainstream actors (male and female) being forced into increasingly sexualised and pornographic roles against their wills. Even some directors are being forced by producers (the guys responsible for a project's business success) to move this direction. Stewart quotes Neil Marshall, *Game of Thrones* director, who was pressured by an HBO executive to put more sex and nudity into an episode of the show.

'It was pretty surreal… This particular exec took me to one side and said, "Look, I represent the pervert side of the audience, okay? Everybody else is the serious drama side - I represent the perv side of the audience, and I'm saying I want full frontal nudity in this scene. So you go uhead and do it."'[212]

So what effect does making entertainment 'for the perv side of the audience' have on our boys and men?

Sociologist, Jill Manning, cites research that pornography consumption is associated with:

- An increased appetite for more graphic types of pornography and sexual activity associated with abusive, illegal or unsafe practices and
- An increasing number of people struggling with compulsive and addictive sexual behaviour

In other words, our pornified media causes boys and men to slide into harder porn, addiction and sex crimes. I mention boys here because a recent Canadian study[213] showed that the average age a boy begins internet porn use today is 10.

10! What does that spell for our future when we consider that researchers have identified the following physical/mental health issues as a result of porn use:

- Erectile dysfunction
- Loss of libido, delayed ejaculation
- Acquiring of fetishes
- Lack of motivation
- Depression
- Social anxiety
- Seeing people as objects
- Brain fog
- ADHD
- 'Real people are boring' syndrome
- Self absorption
- Lack of concentration
- Inability to feel emotions[214]

And these are only the physical and mental health problems that result from porn and pornified media use. What effect is porn having on the *spiritual* health of men and boys? Of girls and women? Of our nation? Of the world?

Actually we don't even have to wait for the future to see what we are in for. The US social action organisation, National Center on Sexual Exploitation, states that child-on-child sexual abuse is increasing dramatically. Not childish sexual play: actual indecent assaults and rape. The organisation also reports that the number one users of child prostitutes in the US are college students.[215]

Our nightmare future is already here.

....

Most of the people who join the porn industry come from broken homes. Many of the girls are sexually abused. So the porn industry actually lures in these kinds of people to exploit them. So basically, when someone is watching pornography, what you're really doing is contributing to the demise and destruction of adult survivors of sexual child abuse who are on drugs and have physical disease. That's really what you are watching because I promise you, nobody in that industry is healthy. Women are lured in, coerced and forced to do sex acts they never agreed to do... [and given] drugs and alcohol to help get through hardcore scenes... The porn industry is modern-day slavery.

— Shelley Lubben: former porn performer and executive director of the Pink Cross Foundation.

The Truth About Porn and Sex Trafficking

The global pornography industry is expected to reach US $100 billion in the near future[216] making it one of the most profitable, and powerful, industries, if not THE most powerful industry. This power enables these mafia-controlled organisations to buy off law enforcement agencies, academic institutions, international corporations and even governments.[217] In 2009 the UN estimated that the global *child* pornography industry alone made a profit of up to $20 billion.[218] To put these figures in perspective, the porn industry generates more annual income than Microsoft, Apple, Google and Amazon combined. These types of earnings could not be realised unless 'massive numbers of male consumers had been conditioned to view women [and children] as objects to be purchased and used.'[219]

Giving Christians disturbing details about the degradation women and children suffer under the porn and sex trade industries is always tricky. One does not want to glorify the horrendous or induce trauma. One, equally, does not want to let this industry get away with saying that what they are selling is harmless. In the introduction to *Big Porn Inc.*, editors Melinda Tankard Reist and Abigail Bray explain why they felt the need to delve into detail about what is going on. [Warning: disturbing details follow]

'We… wanted to correct the pornography industry's distorted version of reality by clearly saying: Here is why you shouldn't believe the myths about pornography being simply "naughty pictures" and "sex between consenting adults" Here is how pornography creates and shapes appetites and demands. Here is how it operates to acclimatise and condition

boys and men to demand the "Porn Star Experience" from women and girls. Here is how men and boys have come to see the "money shot" on a woman's face as the climax to sex. Here is how boys develop a sexual taste for coercion. Here is how they learn predatory sexual attitudes. Here are some possible factors contributing to sex crimes committed by younger men… Here is how men are socialised into eroticising and sexualising children through Pseudo Child Pornography. Here is why demand for child sexual assault images – including babies – is increasing. Here is how women have been turned into "human toilet bowls." Here is how pornography and torture often look the same… In today's mainstream pornography, aggression against women is the rule rather than the exception.[220]

And while porn often gets singled out, because it is the entry point for most people's sexual addictions, the world of sexual dysfunction and injustice doesn't stop there. Rampant porn consumption is fuelling demand for the exploitation of women and girls. According to the United Nations, 2 million children alone are prostituted in the commercial sex trade. The average age of entering into prostitution, world-wide is 14.[221]

In Australia, growing attention is being given to the problem of sex tourism. Sex tourism is when people (usually men) travel to different countries for the purpose of hiring the local prostitutes. Thailand, with its reputation for an infinite supply of male and female prostitutes (including many child prostitutes), and its very lax human rights stand, is a magnet for sex tourists. According to the organisation Positive Aussie Image:

- Approximately 250,000 Western male sex tourists visit Thailand annually
- Some 32,500 are Australians
- Income disparity between Australia and Thailand:
  - » Average Australian adult wages – $1333 per week or $69,316 per annum
  - » Average Thai adult wages – 881 Baht per week ($31.50 AUD) or $1636AUD per annum[222]

In the US, mega-sporting events, like the Super Bowl, have become the scene for mass sexual exploitation. Organised crime rings bring in thousands upon thousands of women[223] and children to the host city to be 'purchased' by men looking for a weekend of sports and 'fun'.

God has blessed us with prosperity and what is being done with it?

> Pornography is contaminating all of our relationships between men and women. The marriage relationship is traumatically damaged and decreased in terms of the emotional intimacy, which is actually the cornerstone of the marriage. —Dr Mary Ann Layden

The Truth About Marriages

Jill Manning (sociologist) has identified these four risks pornography poses to marriage:

- Increased marital distress, and risk of separation and divorce
- Decreased marital intimacy and sexual satisfaction
- Infidelity
- Devaluation of monogamy, marriage and child rearing[224]

In 2002, the American Academy of Matrimonial Lawyers reported the following as the most salient factors present in divorce cases:

- 68% involved one party meeting a new lover over the internet.
- 56% involved one party having 'an obsessive interest in pornographic websites.'

These are cold, hard statistics that hide a world of pain and heartache... heartache of both men and women who have little hope of finding the marital intimacy they long for.

You and I are more than statistics. So are our daughters, sons, granddaughters and grandsons.

> What happens between a husband and a wife matters to the family, the small-group bible study, the church, the community. For Christians, there is no private, sexual sin. — Dr Patricia Weerakoon

What Can be Done?

I was recently listening to an interview with international speaker Tim Bence. Bence has an amazing ministry and incredible walk with God. According to his testimony, he ended up doing the rather big things for the Lord he does today by inviting God into examine him. By repenting. By letting God transform him. In other words, he got himself right.

As part of this process he found his priorities shifting. He found he wanted to be the best husband and best father he possibly could – with God's help. After years of focusing on serving his family and helping them to become all they could be in God, he felt the Lord ask him to pray for his extended family: many of whom did not walk with Him. Within 18 months, they all came to Jesus for salvation and healing.

Not long after that, he felt called to minister to the downtrodden in his city, and the homosexual community, so frequently on the receiving end of Christians' ire… and so on.

The point of this story is that big things begin as we let God straighten *us* out. Then, as we help our family members to become strong in Him. From there: who knows?

Self and Family

If we are the victim of sexual betrayal, the first thing we need to do is heal. No one expects people who have been run over by a truck to get up and start trying to dismantle the vehicle that struck them. Nor do we expect them to prepare dinner that night for their family. We need to be patient with ourselves and seek out the healing we need. We should ask God for the wisdom to know what things we used to do that we could let go of right now. We can also ask Him for the strength to serve in those areas we are still called to. Healing is our number one priority.

If we are still married and our husband is engaged in the healing process, we can enter in. It might not be time to jump in with both feet, but it's never too early to begin praying for him… and for the relationship.

If we are separated, divorced or abandoned, we can still pray for healing for our husband. We can pray (in God's time) for help moving into our forgiveness journey.

As part of our personal and relational healing, we can also tell our story. Not on Facebook. Not on a placard we carry around downtown. But to safe people: in our families, in our churches, in our support groups.

Our story, backed by His Spirit, is one of the greatest tools God has given us to effect change in this world.

> Today's youth may be the most sexually exposed generation in history—and by no coincidence, the first for whom sexuality has become more of a burden than a joy. — Gordon Dalbey

Let's not let some of the stats I quoted scare us into feeling all is lost. God can lead the way in protecting and healing our children (possibly grandchildren) from the effects of our husband's betrayal. Let's ask Him to protect and heal them from the effects of our trauma and from the sin and brokenness of the world.

Then, let's begin talking. If we can't tell them our story (due to their age) we can talk to them about the story of God. The God who loves us. The God who created marriage and has a plan to use it to bless us and others. Older children, and young teens, can be introduced to the concept of appropriate and inappropriate attitudes and behaviours and possibly even sexual sin. If they are in school, there's a good chance they're hearing about it already. Let's not let shame and feelings of discomfort rob us of the opportunity to help equip them for the battle.[225]

Next, we can consider our lifestyle. Are we allowing our story and God's story to be drowned out by the world's story of sex? If media plays a major role in our children's lives, chances are that's what's happening. Why not cut back on – or even, cut out – some (or all) media in the house? Why not consider adding filtering to the TV, computers that are online, and mobile devices? Let's do some research on how to protect our children.[226] Above all, let's ask God for his thoughts on our lifestyle.

To our young men and women, let's be frank about where the world is lying to them. Time may be running short for saving them from a fate like ours. Like our husband's.

Struthers says:

'Does our culture foist a wrong understanding of marriage on men? Men are told to wait until they get their life in order, find the most beautiful woman they can (special attention should be paid to making sure her body maximally arouses him, that is that they have "chemistry"), then somehow woo her to marry him. This view gives too great a weight

to "chemistry" and misses the importance of shared values and commitments. Many marriages built on emotional chemistry that ignore the importance of shared values do not last. After the flames of passion fade, they are left with a mate that doesn't want what they want or value what they value.[227]

Our men – yes even our Christian men – are being set up to be betrayers from the time they are boys. Our girls are being set up to believe infidelity is inevitable and the answer is revenge. However, Struthers offers an antidote to this societal problem:

'For those who chose mates based on shared values and commitments, the chemistry is more than just a flare which quickly goes out. It is a spark which is fanned into a lifelong flame. The result is that sex then images the exclusive love of God for his people.'

That's a story we can happily tell them.

Our Immediate Community

How many women in our church, house group, or Christian women's ministry do we think can relate to what we're going through? The answer would probably shock us. Sometimes it just takes one person willing to talk about sexual addiction and betrayal to open a floodgate of authentic sharing.

If church doesn't feel like the right place, let's ask God to find us others with whom we can talk about these things. It's through vulnerability that intimate relationships are formed. However, as always: let's choose our people prayerfully and wisely.

Once we find people to discuss our hurt and our concerns with, perhaps we can begin to pray together. Pray for each other's healing, pray for the healing of each other's families. Pray for our city.

We can do some research and see if there is a ministry in our city we would like to support. Rahab Ministry, which reaches out to sex workers with the gospel – along with practical help and support – is running in most major centres in Australia. If it's not available in our specific community: let's begin to pray this, or a similar ministry, gets started.

The Nation… and the World

William Wilberforce, famous for leading the slavery abolition movement, once said that God had set two great objects (i.e., 'tasks') before him. The first was the abolition of slavery. The second was 'the reformation of manners' in Britain. That quaint phrase refs to taking action on such issues as child labour, prison reform, alcoholism, and prostitution. In Wilberforce's day (in the 18th century) 25% of single women in London were prostitutes. Their average age was 16.

Wilberforce biographer, Eric Metaxas, writes:

'Suddenly, the idea that women should sell their bodies so that they could feed themselves, or feed their alcohol habit or the alcohol habit of their pimps, could no longer stand. For the first time, in his life, Wilberforce saw the world through God's eyes. But he was living in a culture where almost no one saw things this way. So the task that lay ahead of him was impossible. How would he do it?'[228]

The first answer was God. Wilberforce could not engineer this type of massive change on his own: though he was a popular politician and wealthy man.

On his death bed, John Wesley wrote Wilberforce and warned him that if he was trying to bring about an end to slavery in his own strength he would be 'worn out by the opposition of men and devils. But if God be for you, who can be against you?'[229]

Metaxas expounds on Wesley's warning, saying.

'It was not merely a political or a cultural battle he was undertaking, it was a spiritual battle… to fight something as wicked as the slave trade was to go against an invisible demonic host. God has the power to fight them, but we do not… At its core, every battle worth fighting, is a spiritual battle.'[230]

Metaxas believes that what tipped the scales for Wilberforce was prayer, time spent in scripture and reliance on a solid community of praying brothers and sisters. Moreover, Wilberforce knew he had to win the battle in the cultural sphere, before it could be won in the political sphere.

Thus, Wilberforce set about to use his influence as a cultural icon (due in part to his wealth and connections to the British elite) to 'make goodness fashionable.' One of the ways he did this was by being a conspicuously good husband and father.

To give you an idea of what he was up against, the Prince of Wales – a bigger cultural icon – was famous for being a drunkard who'd had over 7000 sexual conquests.

Over the years, however, Wilberforce – a man motivated by love and famous for showing grace to his opponents – won the battle, with God's help. Slavery was abolished and manners were reformed enough to pave the way for men such as Charles Dickens and other 19th century social reformers.

What can we take away from the story of William Wilberforce?

Do not underestimate the power of prayer and spiritual community.

Do not underestimate the power of love and right living.

Support those on the front lines – which down under includes groups like Collective Shout, Rahab Ministries, and Positive Aussie Image – and go to the front line if you are asked.

But, most of all: never underestimate the power of our risen Lord to stop a worldwide juggernaut.

Taking it Further

- Have you reached out to others now for help and healing? If not, what are the barriers that you see? Have you spoken to God and others about these impediments to getting help?
- Consider asking God about other ways He might want you to grow and heal right now. How might He want you to participate in the healing of your husband, children and other family members?
- Have you considered sharing your story with a small community of trusted believers, or maybe one trusted sister? If not, ask God if that's something He might want you to do at some point. If you get a "Yes!" ask Him to bring the right one to you.
- Are you open to helping other women who have been betrayed, abused or abandoned by unfaithful husbands? Talk to God about how you could do that.
- If you feel you want to do more to help women like yourself, have you considered starting a support group in your area? If you'd like to explore this option, see the resources section at the back of this book under *Resources for Small Groups*.

Endnotes

205 Dalbey, ibid, p. 9.

206 One of the best-selling videogames, played by teens across the western world, *Grand Theft Auto*, rewards players for sleeping with prostitutes and then beating them up.

207 J Reisman, 'The impotence pandemic', WorldNetDaily, Sept. 27, 2007, retrieved Feb. 13, 2013 <http://www.drjudithreisman.com/archives/2007/10/ the_impotence_p_2.html>.

208 MR Brooks, *The Centerfold Syndrome: How Men Can Overcome Objectification and Achieve Intimacy with Women*, Jossy-Bass Publications, 1995.

209 Struthers, ibid, p. 13.

210 G Dines, 'The New Lolita: Pornography and the Sexualization of Childhood', in *Big Porn Inc.*, Spinifex, 2011, p. 3.

211 IACSAS conference, workshop, May 2014.

212 C Stewart, 'Hollywood's Secret Rape Culture, *Happier By Far* (blog), May 20, 2014, retrieved, August 2014 < http://www.capstewart.com/2014/05/hollywoods-secret-rape-culture.html>.

213 *The Independent*, 'Unwelcome Danger of Adolescent Internet Use', Thursday 21 November 2013: <http://www.independent.co.uk/>.

214 *The Independent*, ibid.

215 P Trueman, IACSAS conference, May 2014, Morality in Media (now NCOSE) presentation.

216 E Morss, 'The Economics of the Global Entertainment Industry', June 26, 2009, <http://bit.ly/1s2YpdK> cited from *Big Porn Inc*, p. xiv.

217 ….

218 ….

219 Pure Hope, *Recovery in a Sexualized Culture*, 2013.

220 *Big Porn Inc*. pp. xv-xvi.

221 TIP Report, p. 22, citing UNICEF estimates.

222 D. Martin & S Jones, 'The Social and Reputational Damage Caused by Western and Aussie Sex Tourism in Thailand' *Viewpoint* No. 9, June 2012: p. 26-28.

223 It is estimated that 10,000 women and children were brought in to the city for trafficking for the 2010 event in Miami. This is 10,000 above and beyond the city's own sex workers <http://bit.ly/1HlMZzO>.

224 J Manning: 'Hearing on pornography's impact on marriage & the family,' U.S. Senate Hearing: Subcommittee on the Constitution, Civil Rights and Property Rights, Committee on Judiciary, Nov. 10, 2005.

225 A resource I recommend for children aged 10-14 (with some parental editing depending on the child) is *Growing Up by the Book*, by Patricia Weerakoon. Also, *Good Pictures, Bad Pictures* by Kristen A Jenson.

226 A good article to start with is 'Porn-Proof Your Kids', by the folks at Covenant Eyes: my recommended internet filtering service, <http://bit.ly/1rvWHkY>.

227 Struthers, ibid, ebook p. 309.

228 Eric Metaxas, *7 Men: and the Secret of their Greatness*, Thomas Nelson, April 30, 2013, p. 46.

229 Metaxas, ibid. p. 47.

230 Metaxas, ibid, p. 48.

Resources

FOR WIVES

Online Resources

Beyond Betrayal blog: www.beyondbetrayal.community
Redemptive Living for Women: www.rlforwomen.com
Paula Hall and Associates: www.paulahall.co.uk
Porn and Your Husband – Covenant Eyes PDF: http://www.covenanteyes.com/resources/wifes-guide/
Daily Strength: online support for families of sex offenders – www.dailystrength.org/groups/families-of-sex-offenders

Books

Your Sexually Addicted Spouse, Dr Barbara Steffans, Marsha Means
Spouses of Sex Addicts: Hope for the Journey, Richard Blankenship
Boundaries: When to Say Yes, How to Say No, Dr Henry Cloud, Dr John Townsend

Resources for Small Groups

Door of Hope: facilitator training workbook, DM Dixon
Rescued: A Woman's Guide to Surviving and Thriving After Sexual Betrayal , Shelly Martinkus
Journey to Healing and Joy workbook, Marsha Means
Boundaries: When to Say Yes, How to Say No workbook, Dr John Townsend
The Trauma Recovery Group, Michaela Mendelsohn and Judith Lewis Herman
Beyond Betrayal: www.beyondbetrayal.community

Small Group Contact Information (Australia/New Zealand)

Queensland, Australia – Amanda Jackson: jackson.amanda4@gmail.com
South Island, New Zealand – Bianca Margetts: waimakgirl@hotmail.com
North Island, New Zealand – Lisa Taylor: beyondbetrayalblog@gmail.com

Therapists and Coaches

A Circle of Joy: www.acircleofjoy.com
Redemptive Living for Women: rlforwomen.com
Living Truth: www.living-truth.org

Life Works: www.lifeworksms.com
Safe Passages: www.safepassagescounseling.com
Where there has been sex offending/incest:
Marcella Burns – marcellaburns@yahoo.com

Suicide Prevention Hotlines
Lifeline: 13 11 14 - https://www.lifeline.org.au
Lifeline Aotearoa: 09 909 8750 - http://www.lifeline.org.nz

FOR ADDICTS

Online
IACSAS therapist directory: www.sexaddictioncertification.org/find-a-specialist/
Paula Hall and Associates: www.paulahall.co.uk
Samson Society: www.samsonsociety.com
Porn to Purity: porntopurity.com
Proven Men: www.provenmen.org
Pure Intimacy: www.pureintimacy.org
Integrity Restored: www.integrityrestored.com

Books
Wired for Intimacy: How Pornography Hijacks the Male Brain, Dr William Struthers
Surfing for God, Michael J Cusick
Worthy of Her Trust: What You Need to Do to Rebuild Trust and Win Her Back, Jason Martinkus and Steve Arterburn
Every Man's Battle, Fred Stoeker and Steve Arterburn
Samson and the Pirate Monks, Nate Larkin
Loving People: How to Love and Be Loved, Dr John Townsend
Sons of the Father, Gordon Dalbey

FOR THE COUPLE

Online
Remptive Living: Kitchen convo series: redemptiveliving.com/access-kitchen-convos/
New Life TV: tv.newlife.com
Pure Intimacy: pureintimacy.org

Books

Worthy of Her Trust: What You Need to Do to Rebuild Trust and Win Her Back, Jason Martinkus and Steve Arterburn

Boundaries in Marriage, Dr John Townsend

Pure Sex: The Spirituality of Sexual Desire, Gordon Dalbey

The Best Sex for Life, Patricia Weerakoon

Reclaiming Paradise, Steve Farnworth: email to request a copy: stevefarnworth55@gmail.com

FOR CHILDREN AND YOUTH

Online

Fortify: www.fortifyprogram.org

Secret Keeper Girl: secretkeepergirl.com

The Porn Effect: www.porneffect.com

Books

Good Pictures, Bad Pictures: Kristen A Jensen and Gail Poyner

Who Moved the Goal Post?: Dan Gresh

Get Lost: Your Guide to finding True Love, Dannah Gresh

Every Young Man's Battle (where addiction already exists), Fred Stoeker and Steve Arterburn

Growing Up by the Book (ages 10-14), Patricia Weerakoon

Teen Sex (ages 14 +), Patricia Weerakoon

FOR CLERGY

Sex Addicts in Ministry: www.sainministry.org

Missionaries to Ministers: www.missionariestoministers.com

Covenant Eyes: "Fight Porn in Your Church" free PDF booklet

Pure Intimacy: www.pureintimacy.org

Integrity Restored: www.integrityrestored.com

FOR THERAPISTS AND COACHES

IACSAS: www.sexaddictioncertification.org

APSATS: apsats.org

FOR SOCIAL ACTION

National Center on Sexual Exploitation: endsexualexploitation.org
Rahab Ministry: rahabministry.org
Collective Shout: www.collectiveshout.org
International Justice Mission: www.ijm.org

FOR RESEARCH

Covenant Eyes Pornography Statistics
Big Porn Inc
IWF: Internet Watch Foundation: www.iwf.org.uk
Proven Men: www.provenmen.org

About the Author

Lisa is an award-winning author, mother of three, and trauma survivor living in New Zealand. As a young-adult novelist, Lisa incorporates the themes of media-awareness, maturity and healthy sexuality into her stories (see motivegamesbook.com). As a non-fiction author she writes on issues related to women's/children's healing from sexual addiction and betrayal.

Lisa and her husband, M, facilitate sex-addiction-related support groups in New Zealand's Northland. They also speak to youth groups about healthy sexuality, and to Christian organisations about sexual addiction and partner trauma.

In 2015, Lisa and M became certified pastoral sex addiction specialists (International Association of Sex Addiction Specialists) and Lisa is also a trained support-group facilitator (A Circle of Joy Ministries). She shares the results of her research, relevant resources, and thoughts about the journey at *Beyond Betrayal Community:* www.beyondbetrayal.community

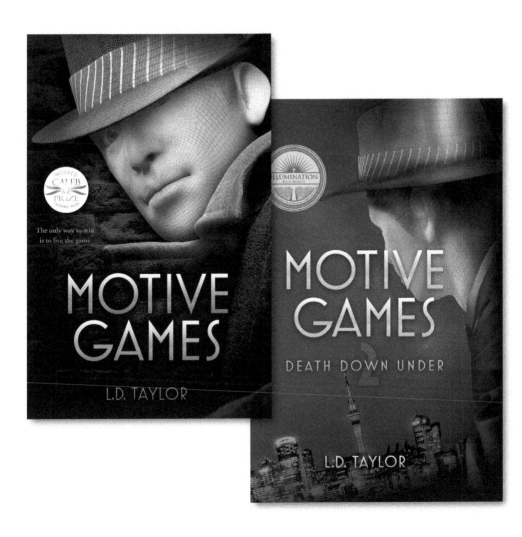

The award-winning Motive Games series gives teens (aged 13-19) a fast-paced, high-tech mystery with heart and soul. Though set in the videogame industry, the stories get teens thinking about what kinds of values the entertainment industry is promoting, and how those values may contrast with a Christian worldview. Some of the many themes explored include: creating vs consuming, hope vs. despair and protecting women vs. using women. For more: www.motivegamesbook.com

Lightning Source UK Ltd.
Milton Keynes UK
UKHW022213200820
368567UK00012B/2961